New Directions for
Child and Adolescent
Development

Lene Arnett Jensen
Reed W. Larson
EDITORS-IN-CHIEF

William Damon
FOUNDING EDITOR

Youth Civic Development: Work at the Cutting Edge

Constance A. Flanagan

Brian D. Christens

EDITORS

Number 134 • Winter 2011
Jossey-Bass
San Francisco

YOUTH CIVIC DEVELOPMENT: WORK AT THE CUTTING EDGE
Constance A. Flanagan, Brian D. Christens (eds.)
New Directions for Child and Adolescent Development, no. 134
Lene Arnett Jensen, Reed W. Larson, Editors-in-Chief

Microfilm copies of issues and articles are available in 16mm and 35mm,
as well as microfiche in 105mm, through University Microfilms, Inc.,
300 North Zeeb Road, Ann Arbor, Michigan 48106-1346.

ISSN 1520-3247   electronic ISSN 1534-8687

NEW DIRECTIONS FOR CHILD AND ADOLESCENT DEVELOPMENT is part of The
Jossey-Bass Education Series and is published quarterly by Wiley
Subscription Services, Inc., a Wiley company, at Jossey-Bass, One
Montgomery Street, Suite 1200, San Francisco, CA 94104-4594. Periodi-
cals postage paid at San Francisco, California, and at additional mailing
offices. Postmaster: Send address changes to New Directions for Child and
Adolescent Development, Jossey-Bass, One Montgomery Street, Suite
1200, San Francisco, CA 94104-4594.

New Directions for Child and Adolescent Development is indexed in Cam-
bridge Scientific Abstracts (CSA/CIG), CHID: Combined Health Infor-
mation Database (NIH), Contents Pages in Education (T&F), Current
Abstracts (EBSCO), Educational Research Abstracts Online (T&F),
EMBASE/Excerpta Medica (Elsevier), ERIC Database (Education
Resources Information Center), Index Medicus/MEDLINE/PubMed
(NLM), Linguistics & Language Behavior Abstracts (CSA/CIG), Psycho-
logical Abstracts/PsycINFO (APA), Social Services Abstracts (CSA/CIG),
SocINDEX (EBSCO), and Sociological Abstracts (CSA/CIG).

SUBSCRIPTION rates: For the U.S., $89 for individuals and $343 for institutions. Please see ordering information page at end of journal.

EDITORIAL CORRESPONDENCE should be e-mailed to the editors-in-chief:
Lene Arnett Jensen (ljensen@clarku.edu) and Reed W. Larson (larsonr@
illinois.edu).

Jossey-Bass Web address: www.josseybass.com

Contents

1. Youth Civic Development: Historical Context and   1
Emerging Issues
Constance A. Flanagan, Brian D. Christens
The authors provide a brief history of youth civic development as
an area of study and, through a summary of the contributions of the
chapters in this volume, discuss emerging issues.

2. The Developmental Roots of Social Responsibility in   11
Childhood and Adolescence
Laura Wray-Lake, Amy K. Syvertsen
The authors posit that the development of social responsibility begins
in childhood and develops in adolescence as a value orientation that
links one's own fate with those of fellow human beings.

3. Taking Stock of Youth Organizing: An Interdisciplinary   27
Perspective
Brian D. Christens, Ben Kirshner
Integrating literature from multiple disciplines, the authors provide a
multilevel framework for understanding a promising model for civic
development and social change—youth organizing.

4. Critical Consciousness: Current Status and Future   43
Directions
Roderick J. Watts, Matthew A. Diemer, Adam M. Voight
Drawing on the work of the Brazilian educator Paulo Freire, the
authors explicate the role of critical consciousness in youth civic
development.

5. "Unapologetic and Unafraid": Immigrant Youth Come Out   59
From the Shadows
Hinda Seif
The author explores the changing political consciousness and action of
Latino/a youth as they organize and publicly advocate for equal rights
and an end to discrimination against members of their ethnic group.

6. Early Educational Foundations for the Development of   77
Civic Responsibility: An African Experience
Robert Serpell, Paul Mumba, Tamara Chansa-Kabali
The authors describe an innovative peer education curriculum in rural
Zambia that not only promotes health, but also fosters cooperation,
gender equality, and social responsibility.

7. Youth Civic Development: Theorizing a Domain With
Evidence From Different Cultural Contexts 95
Constance A. Flanagan, M. Loreto Martínez, Patricio Cumsille,
Tsakani Ngomane
The authors point toward the primacy of collective action, groupways,
and mediating institutions as aspects of the civic domain germane to
youth development across cultures.

INDEX 111

Flanagan, C. A., & Christens, B. D. (2011). Youth civic development: Historical context and emerging issues. In C. A. Flanagan & B. D. Christens (Eds.), Youth civic development: Work at the cutting edge. *New Directions for Child and Adolescent Development, 134*, 1–9.

1

Youth Civic Development: Historical Context and Emerging Issues

Constance A. Flanagan, Brian D. Christens

Abstract

The civic domain has taken its place in the scholarship and practice of youth development. From the beginning, the field has focused on youth as assets who contribute to the common good of their communities. Work at the cutting edge of this field integrates research and practice and focuses on the civic incorporation of groups who often have been marginalized from mainstream society. The body of work also extends topics of relevance to human development by considering themes of justice, social responsibility, critical consciousness, and collective action. © 2011 Wiley Periodicals, Inc.

New Directions for Child and Adolescent Development, no. 134, Winter 2011 © Wiley Periodicals, Inc.
Published online in Wiley Online Library (wileyonlinelibrary.com). • DOI: 10.1002/cd.307

1

O ver the past few decades, there has been a growing awareness of the civic/political domain as a context for adolescent and youth development. Signs that this field has come of age include the formation of CIRCLE (www.civicyouth.org), a national research organization and clearinghouse on youth civic engagement and the publication of the first *Handbook of Research on Civic Engagement in Youth* (Sherrod, Torney-Purta, & Flanagan, 2010). In addition, two prominent international reports on youth in the majority world devoted chapters to citizenship. Both *Growing Up Global: The Changing Transitions to Adulthood in Developing Countries* (Lloyd, 2005) issued by the National Research Council and Institute of Medicine's Committee on Population and *World Development Report: Development and the Next Generation* issued by the World Bank (2007) considered the civic engagement of younger generations important in its own right, but also critical for the health of communities, economies, governments, and societies.

An Evolving Field

Scholarly interest in the civic/political domain had been increasing in North America and Western Europe, in part, due to concerns that recent cohorts of young adults had become disengaged from politics and civic life, and that the community organizations that ushered younger generations into civic/political life were on the decline (Putnam, 2000). Consequently, attention turned to the developmental precursors of adult political engagement and to a definition of civic life that expanded beyond electoral politics.

From its inception, this field involved practitioners and scholars from multiple disciplines, most notably, education, youth development, political science, and psychology. Besides its multidisciplinary character, it also was a field that believed in the reciprocal relationship between theory and practice. In this regard, the contributions of two bodies of scholarship are especially noteworthy. Research on positive youth development (PYD) and on service learning/community service both have focused attention on the contributions that young people make to their communities (Benson, Scales, Hamilton, & Sesma, 2006; Furco & Root, 2010). These fields have contributed to our understanding of youth as assets to their communities and as agents of social change; they also have pointed to the opportunities for civic engagement in the contexts where young people spend time. Research on civic education and on extracurricular and community-based organizations has complemented this scholarship.

What have we learned? First, youth are more likely to be civically active as adults if they have had opportunities during adolescence to work collaboratively with peers and adults on engaging issues and to discuss current events with parents, teachers, and peers. Interest in political issues tends to be generated by controversy, contestation, discussion, and the perception that it matters to take a stand. Second, young people's sense of social incorporation (solidarity with others, identification with community institutions, being respected and heard by adults) is a psychological factor that is positively related to youth assuming social responsibility for others in their communities and for taking civic actions (e.g., voting and volunteering) in young adulthood. These relationships are true for youth from different social class and ethnic backgrounds. Third, there is a class and racial divide in the civic opportunities available to young people: cumulative disadvantage built up over the years of pre-school through twelfth grade (including the lack of opportunities to practice civic skills, the competing demands on attention and time of living in economically stressed communities, and especially events such as dropping out of school or getting arrested) depresses civic incorporation and civic action later in life. Fourth, besides opportunities, there are traits of personality (e.g., extraversion, confidence, optimism) that predispose some youth to join organizations and get engaged in civic action. Fifth, youth engagement in meaningful civic projects is positively associated with their psychosocial well-being and mental health.

This volume of *New Directions for Child and Adolescent Development* builds on the extant body of work and pushes the boundaries in cutting-edge theoretical, empirical, and practical directions. Like the PYD and service learning paradigms, the focus is on youth as assets, acting in the broader and best interests of their communities. Nevertheless, contributors to the volume press beyond these paradigms by raising issues of social justice and unequal access to society's resources for groups of youth who are marginalized from the mainstream. Further, besides identifying inequalities in access, the authors expound on ways that young people are contesting those injustices by taking action. Moreover, several chapters focus on groups of youth who often have been left out of the literature on youth civic engagement. Three chapters focus in particular on the political/civic actions of youth in the United States who are marginalized due to their social class, ethnic minority, or immigrant status. Two others draw from research on youth in the majority world.

The volume also makes cutting-edge contributions to theory in this field and in the broader field of adolescent development, in part because contributors have extended the boundaries of questions to ask, and of groups of young people to include in answering them. The lens is on the value of collective action and commitment to a common good for adolescent development. In itself, this is a departure from the more common emphasis on individual and interpersonal relationships in the field of youth development.

Organization of the Volume

Laura Wray-Lake and Amy Syvertsen open the volume with a chapter on the developmental origins of social responsibility in childhood and adolescence. This value orientation, which is based on empathy with others, transcends self-interest and links one's well-being and fate with those of fellow human beings. Thus, social responsibility refers to obligations for our common good or shared self-interest with fellow citizens and human beings. Arguing that this value orientation is at the heart of civic/political action, Wray-Lake and Syvertsen trace its developmental foundations to socialization that emphasizes principles of care and justice and that respects children's rights to participate in democratic decision making. Socialization practices such as modeling prosocial action (e.g., parents' own involvement in community action) or emphasizing standards of concern or care for others when communicating with children nurture socially responsible children and adolescents.

In the next chapter Brian Christens and Ben Kirshner provide an integrative and historical analysis of the interdisciplinary field of youth organizing. They trace the evolution of this field that from the beginning was attentive to the insights and the anger of young people who were marginalized from mainstream institutions. The authors characterize the field of youth organizing as a combination of community organizing, with its emphasis on ordinary people working collectively to advance shared interests, and positive youth development, with its emphasis on asset-based approaches to working with young people. Based on an impressive body of scholarship employing different theoretical perspectives, Christens and Kirshner identify common elements of this form of youth civic engagement including relationship development, popular education, social action, and participatory research and evaluation. In just a little over a decade, youth organizing has evolved from an innovative, but marginal model to one that is widely recognized, respected, and adopted by community-based youth development organizations.

In the next chapter on critical consciousness, Roderick Watts, Matthew Diemer, and Adam Voight also apply a historical lens by locating the theoretical origins of this approach to youth political development in Paulo Freire's classic work in Brazil. The capacities of people—regardless of their background or education—to analyze their society and their place in it is the process of becoming conscious, as Freire advocated. Not surprisingly, issues of social justice emerge when it is the powerless who participate in this process. However, awareness is only the beginning. According to Watts, Diemer, and Voight, besides critical reflection, critical action and political efficacy are core components of critical consciousness as an approach to youth political development.

The political consciousness and action of Latina/o immigrants is the subject of the next chapter. Author Hinda Seif illustrates several ways in which attention to the political activities of this group enrich the field of youth civic engagement. First, although undocumented immigrants are, in principle, the object of anti-immigrant discourse and policies, discrimination also is leveled at Latina/os who are citizens of the United States or legal residents because of their shared cultural/ethnic identity. Thus, Latina/o youth, regardless of their legal status, have a vested interest in a shared political cause. Second, attention to the forms that immigrants' engagement takes expands the concept of civic participation. Although immigrant youth may not be eligible to vote, many volunteer in their communities and mediate between their cultural group and mainstream culture, often interpreting policy and the law for older members of their ethnic group. The high level of young Latina/o participation in protests against anti-immigrant legislation belies assertions that they are politically disengaged. Finally, Seif raises a developmental argument about the dawning of political consciousness in this group. Whereas they are guaranteed rights to public education in childhood, they are excluded from other routes to citizenship upon graduation from high school. Attaining the American dream via access to education has become the political cause uniting Latina/o youth and lobbying for DREAM legislation has resulted in many becoming political leaders, symbols for younger and older co-ethnics.

The last two chapters move beyond the United States. First, Robert Serpell, Paul Mumba, and Tamara Chansa-Kabali describe an innovative elementary curriculum in a rural community in Zambia and document the long-term impact on social responsibility in young adulthood. The Child-to-Child (CtC) curriculum focuses on health education and practices that enable children to assume responsibility for the health of younger peers. President Kenneth Kaunda officially launched the program in Zambia with a call for all children to consider themselves champions of people's health. The curriculum builds on the common practices of many African cultures of assigning children responsibilities for the community early in life. Mumba describes the democratic practices that he adopted as a teacher of the CtC curriculum including mixed-gender peer groups that emphasized interdependence in learning; gender neutrality in the allocation of tasks and leadership; group collaboration and evaluations based on group performance, which encouraged faster learners to help slower students; children's rights to voice and to disagree with one another; and opportunities for contributing to the nurturant care of younger children and for engagement in public service. The authors end their chapter with a summary of their follow-up research with young adults seventeen years after completing the CtC program. Participants reported that involvement in CtC promoted their personal agency, cooperative disposition, attitudes toward gender equality, and civic responsibility in early adulthood.

The volume closes with a chapter by Constance Flanagan, M. Loreto Martinez, Patricio Cumsille, and Tsakani Ngomane. Drawing from studies and historical events in many parts of the majority world, these authors argue that there are certain universal aspects of the civic domain in youth development. These include the primacy of collective action for forming political identities and ideas and the greater heterogeneity of encounters in the civic when compared to other activity domains; the *groupways* or accumulated opportunities for acting over the course of childhood and adolescence due to the groups (cultural, gender, social class, caste, etc.) to which a young person belongs; and the role of mediating institutions (schools, community-based organizations, etc.) as spaces where the younger generation's collective actions contribute to political stability and change. The authors argue that theory in the broader field of youth development could be enriched by systematically attending to these common elements of the civic domain.

Conclusion

The chapters in this volume have in common a set of understandings that are drawn from the contemporary scholarship on positive youth development and civic engagement. For example, all of the authors embrace perspectives on young people as societal assets that should be supported to develop to their greatest potential, rather than treated as latent problems or sheltered from interactions with their communities. All of the authors argue for more intergenerational and inclusive public policies and practices in community and organizational settings. Moreover, all authors share the perspective that societies are enhanced when young people are able to participate and contribute in meaningful ways. These core understandings have been steadily gaining wider acceptance, not only in the study of childhood, adolescence, and emerging adulthood, but also in practice across many fields and settings.

However, the chapters in this volume also go further by pointing to emerging directions within the young field of youth civic development. Drawing out the various strands from this issue, we believe that there are cases to be made for several pertinent and emerging directions for theory, research, and action. First, issues of justice and power continue to dwell at the margins of the larger discussions on positive youth development and the most prevalent models for youth civic engagement (e.g., service learning, volunteering). More of these models, and more of the empirical and theoretical work on positive youth development, should consider the implications of systematic injustices and the possibilities for building power among marginalized groups and solidarity across lines of difference. Second, the majority world should feature more prominently in research on youth civic development—for theory's sake, if not for the simple reason that the majority world is home to the vast majority of young people. Third, the challenges faced by marginalized populations in both the majority and minority worlds should become the focus of more action-oriented work on positive youth development and civic engagement. Growing inequalities mean that the need is ever greater for models that engage young people in the task of addressing social and political challenges through democratic

NEW DIRECTIONS FOR CHILD AND ADOLESCENT DEVELOPMENT • DOI: 10.1002/cd

action. More of the research on youth development and civic engagement should meet these challenges head on (Watts & Flanagan, 2007).

The contributions of the volume to theory also derive from the fact that the authors take seriously Kurt Lewin's (1951) commitment to action research and his appreciation that both theory and practice are enriched when scholars and practitioners collaborate in defining the questions and methods of inquiry. Lewin's observation is now six decades old but still resonates today:

> Many psychologists working today in an applied field are keenly aware of the need for close cooperation between theoretical and applied psychology. This can be accomplished in psychology, as it has been accomplished in physics, if the theorist does not look toward applied problems with high-brow aversion or with a fear of social problems, and if the applied psychologist realizes that there is nothing so practical as a good theory. (p. 169)

The intimate connection between theory and practice is a common denominator in these chapters. For example, youth organizing is based on an integration of community-based practice with scholarship and analysis of the practice. Theory about social change in the gender attitudes of young adults in Zambia emerges from a careful analysis of the practice in the CtC curriculum that tried to change those attitudes.

Through this interconnected view of research and practice, the chapters in this volume also identify applications to practice. These are relevant across the full spectrum of youth-oriented and intergenerational settings (e.g., educational institutions, after-school programs, nonprofit organizations) and the policies that support this work. Critical consciousness (Watts, Diemer & Voight, this volume) and social responsibility (Wray-Lake & Syvertsen, this volume) provide two conceptual anchor points for practice. In addition, both concepts represent potential target outcomes for youth programming and education. Experiential education and participatory action research are two of the most promising mechanisms for developing social responsibility and critical consciousness. Examples of programs and settings that incorporate these mechanisms include youth organizing initiatives like those described by Christens and Kirshner, youth-led curricula like the CtC curriculum described in the chapter by Serpell, Mumba, and Chansa-Kabali, and involvement in social movements like the young leaders organizing for immigrant rights described in the chapter by Seif. Further, the more common settings that youth inhabit (e.g., schools, sports teams, and other extracurricular activities) can become more explicit in their intent to cultivate civic development including social responsibility and critical consciousness.

Besides practice, theories of youth development also are enriched by attention to the civic domain. As Flanagan, Martinez, Cumsille, and Ngomane discuss, there are universal aspects of this domain that transcend particular polities and cultures. Scholarly attention to the collective actions of young people working to make their schools or their nations more inclusive may yield new insights into ways that people fulfill the human need to belong. Exposure to more heterogeneous people and perspectives through civic action may enhance adolescents' intellectual and reflective capacities. Moreover, understanding why young people engage in civic work may expand theories of motivation and purpose. In particular, attention to the civic actions of young people who are all too often absent from research should expand our paradigms of youth development and the way we frame our inquiries. This volume of *New Directions in Child and Adolescent Development* signifies that youth civic engagement has come of age as an important domain of youth development. Nonetheless, in its relatively short life span, the field has evolved and the future is wide open.

References

Benson, P. L., Scales, P. C., Hamilton, S. F., & Sesma Jr., A. (2006). Positive youth development: Theory, research, and applications. In W. Damon & R. M. Lerner (Eds.), *Handbook of child psychology. Vol. 1. Theoretical models of human development* (6th ed., pp. 894–941). Hoboken, NJ: Wiley.

Christens, B. D., & Kirshner, B. (2011). Taking stock of youth organizing: An interdisciplinary perspective. In C. A. Flanagan & B. D. Christens (Eds.), Youth civic development: Work at the cutting edge. *New Directions for Child and Adolescent Development, 134,* 27–41.

Flanagan, C. A., Martinez, M. L., Cumsille, P., & Ngomane, T. (2011). Youth civic development: Theorizing a domain with evidence from different cultural contexts. In C. A. Flanagan & B. D. Christens (Eds.), Youth civic development: Work at the cutting edge. *New Directions for Child and Adolescent Development, 134,* 95–109.

Furco, A., & Root, S. (2010). Research demonstrates the value of service learning. *Phi Delta Kappan, 91*(5), 16–20. Retrieved from http://www.pdkintl.org/kappan/index.htm.

Lewin, K. (1951). *Field theory in social science: Selected theoretical papers,* D. Cartwright (Ed.). New York, NY: Harper & Row. (Original work published 1944)

Lloyd, C. B. (Ed.). (2005). *Growing up global: The changing transitions to adulthood in developing countries.* Washington, DC: National Academies Press.

Putnam, R. (2000). *Bowling alone: The collapse and revival of American community.* New York, NY: Simon and Schuster.

Seif, H. (2011). "Unapologetic and unafraid": Immigrant youth come out from the shadows. In C. A. Flanagan & B. D. Christens (Eds.), Youth civic development: Work at the cutting edge. *New Directions for Child and Adolescent Development, 134,* 59–75.

Serpell, R., Mumba, P., & Chansa-Kabali, T. (2011). Early educational foundations for the development of civic responsibility: An African experience. In C. A. Flanagan & B. D. Christens (Eds.), Youth civic development: Work at the cutting edge. *New Directions for Child and Adolescent Development, 134,* 77–93.

Sherrod, L., Torney-Purta, J., & Flanagan, C. (Eds.). (2010). *Handbook of research on civic engagement in youth.* Hoboken, NJ: Wiley.

Watts, R. J., Diemer, M. A., & Voight, A. M. (2011). Critical consciousness: Current status and future directions. In C. A. Flanagan & B. D. Christens (Eds.), Youth civic development: Work at the cutting edge. *New Directions for Child and Adolescent Development, 134*, 43–57.

Watts, R. J., & Flanagan, C. (2007). Pushing the envelope on youth civic engagement: A developmental and liberation psychology perspective. *Journal of Community Psychology, 35*(6), 779–792. doi:10.1002/jcop.20178

World Bank. (2007). *World development report 2007: Development and the next generation*. Washington, DC: Author.

Wray-Lake, L., & Syvertsen, A. K. (2011). The developmental roots of social responsibility in childhood and adolescence. In C. A. Flanagan & B. D. Christens (Eds.), Youth civic development: Work at the cutting edge. *New Directions for Child and Adolescent Development, 134*, 11–25.

CONSTANCE A. FLANAGAN *is professor of human ecology at the University of Wisconsin–Madison. E-mail: caflanagan@wisc.edu*

BRIAN D. CHRISTENS *is assistant professor of human ecology at the University of Wisconsin–Madison. E-mail: bchristens@wisc.edu*

Wray-Lake, L., & Syvertsen, A. K. (2011). The developmental roots of social responsibility in childhood and adolescence. In C. A. Flanagan & B. D. Christens (Eds.), Youth civic development: Work at the cutting edge. *New Directions for Child and Adolescent Development*, 134, 11–25.

2

The Developmental Roots of Social Responsibility in Childhood and Adolescence

Laura Wray-Lake, Amy K. Syvertsen

Abstract

Social responsibility is a value orientation, rooted in democratic relationships with others and moral principles of care and justice, that motivates certain civic actions. Given its relevance for building stronger relationships and communities, the development of social responsibility within individuals should be a more concerted focus for developmental scholars and youth practitioners. During childhood and adolescence, the developmental roots of individuals' social responsibility lie in the growth of executive function, empathy and emotion regulation, and identity. Efforts to cultivate children and adolescents' social responsibility in the proximal settings of their everyday lives should emphasize modeling prosocial behaviors, communicating concerns for others, and creating opportunities to practice civic skills. © 2011 Wiley Periodicals, Inc.

C hildren and adolescents are capable of making positive contributions to society, and developmental experiences during this time
also set the stage for citizenship across the life span. Social responsibility, a sense of duty or obligation to contribute to the greater good, is a
personal value that manifests itself in our beliefs and the way we live with
others (Berman, 1997; Gallay, 2006; Kohlberg & Candee, 1984). In developmental science, social responsibility conceptually overlaps with a range
of constructs such as moral development, empathy, altruism, and prosocial values and behaviors. Responsibility implies feeling accountable for
one's decisions and actions, reliable and dependable to others, and empowered to act on issues within one's control. As such, socially responsible
individuals are active agents in their development, imbued with a duty to
act on moral and prosocial grounds. As an outgrowth of the already rich
literatures on prosocial, moral, cognitive, and identity development, social
responsibility is at the cutting edge of developmental science because of
its emphasis on responsibility and direct implications for positive social
change through the cultivation of values and actions.

To be intentional about cultivating social responsibility within individuals, we first need to know what it is and how it develops. In this chapter, we focus on personal and environmental characteristics in childhood
and adolescence that undergird the promotion of social responsibility. Our
aims are threefold. First, we define social responsibility in terms of development while emphasizing core elements that are shared across theoretical
traditions. Second, grounded in a developmental perspective, we seek to
identify aspects of childhood and adolescence that represent opportunities
for growth in social responsibility. Third, we turn to contexts, focusing on
the proximal settings of youth's everyday lives that encourage social
responsibility.

Defining Social Responsibility

Social responsibility is a concept used across the fields of business, economics, political science, and positive psychology. Across disciplines,
social responsibility is defined as reflecting concerns that extend beyond
personal wants, needs, or gains (Gallay, 2006). Adopting a developmental
lens, we consider social responsibility to be a *value* orientation that motivates individuals' prosocial, moral, and civic behaviors. Relationships with
others and a moral sense of care and justice are central to our definition of
social responsibility.

Social Responsibility as a Value. Values are broad personal priori-
ties, with a cognitive as well as an emotional component, that guide specific beliefs, attitudes, and behaviors. As a core aspect of the self, values
give coherence to personal identities and make actions more purposeful
(Hitlin, 2003). Social responsibility traverses the value types of universalism (e.g., justice) and benevolence (e.g., helping close others) that both

fall under the broader value dimension of self-transcendence (Schwartz, 1992). Thus, framed as a value, social responsibility offers important insights into how individuals view themselves in relation to others, where "others" can be broadly extended to the welfare of unknown others, society, other species, and the environment or refer more locally to caring for friends and family.

Social responsibility values are expected to motivate a person's behaviors that involve helping others and contributing to society. For example, values prioritizing the greater good have been positively associated with community service (Pratt, Hunsberger, Pancer, & Alisat, 2003), pro-environmental behaviors (Verplanken & Holland, 2002), and political activism (Mayton & Furnham, 1994). Civic engagement can have myriad motivations, but in accordance with current conceptualizations (Zaff, Boyd, Li, Lerner, & Lerner, 2010), we argue that only those civic actions motivated by care and justice fall under the umbrella of social responsibility. Furthermore, a person's civic behaviors and social responsibility are mutually influential: just as social responsibility may provoke civic action, certain kinds of civic actions may enhance social responsibility. Yet, values do not always lead to action. Numerous obstacles prevent youth from acting on social responsibility, such as time constraints, stress related to meeting one's own basic needs, social norms that emphasize competition rather than concern for others, or lack of opportunity. These obstacles should be addressed, where possible, to enable equal opportunity for exercising social responsibility regardless of one's situation or social background.

Relationships with Others. Humans have a fundamental need to belong to something larger than themselves (Baumeister & Leary, 1995). Likewise, one's social responsibility is rooted in relationships with others, meaning that individuals must feel connected to others and see oneself as part of a larger entity before their responsibility extends beyond the self. When supported by others, growing autonomy during adolescence can also foster social responsibility, as autonomy entails having agency to act on one's values. When people identify with a group, they are more inclined to forgo self-interests to benefit others and come to the aid of group members (see Syvertsen, Flanagan, & Stout, 2009). Common bonds established in social relationships engender feelings of reciprocity to contribute to one's community and beyond.

Reciprocity is more likely when relationships are founded on mutual respect and trust. When young people feel like they have equal membership and rights within a group and that their voices are heard, they are more likely to feel responsible for their community and society writ large (Flanagan, Cumsille, Gill, & Gallay, 2007). Trust in humanity is a developmental foundation for social responsibility and can prompt civic contributions (Flanagan, 2003). In other words, certain kinds of relationships—rooted in equality, mutual respect for opinions, and

NEW DIRECTIONS FOR CHILD AND ADOLESCENT DEVELOPMENT • DOI: 10.1002/cd

trust—breed social responsibility. The extent to which social responsibility broadens to include unknown others may depend on trust and experiences in interactions with diverse others.

Morality: Care and Justice. Moral principles of care and justice are central to social responsibility (Berman, 1997). When considered in concert, these principles allow individuals to balance compassion for those in need with concerns of fairness and equality (Gilligan, 1982)—a combination that reflects the emotional (e.g., empathy, compassion) and cognitive (e.g., justice reasoning) components of social responsibility. Caring and justice are distinct, but compatible principles.

Social responsibility overlaps with developmental constructs like altruism, prosocial behavior, and care reasoning. The core component of these concepts is a concern for others. Many character education programs advance a care perspective of social responsibility through emphasis on compassion, prosocial skills, and integrity; such curricula tend to cultivate citizens who obey laws, donate to a cause when asked, or volunteer to help people in need (Westheimer & Kahne, 2004). Thus, a care orientation without a justice lens may result in social responsibility that reflects loyalty and obedience.

Compared to caring, justice is perhaps a more complex moral principle as it entails reasoning about fairness in how resources and punishments should be allocated. Cognitive developmental theory suggests that moral reasoning parallels cognitive development, with reasoning about justice and rights becoming increasingly complex and abstract with age (Kohlberg, 1981). Though the concept is not explicitly political, social responsibility may be a developmental foundation for political views and actions (Flanagan & Tucker, 1999), and a justice orientation may be the link that connects social responsibility to the political realm. For example, youth in the United Students Against Sweatshops organization engage in protests for fair labor laws across the globe, a goal that entails little personal gain for students themselves (Ballinger, 2006). From a liberation psychology perspective, social responsibility involves promoting social justice and challenging oppressive power structures (Watts & Flanagan, 2007). Given that a justice orientation entails an understanding that people are entitled to certain rights and should be treated accordingly, social responsibility may go beyond loyalty and obedience and evoke a drive to challenge injustice.

Development in Childhood and Adolescence

Social responsibility is a prosocial value orientation, rooted in democratic relationships with others and moral principles of care and justice, that motivates a range of civic actions. This integrated definition of social responsibility sets the stage for examining relevant developmental domains that shape social responsibility. We highlight several aspects of emotional, cognitive, and identity development that may precede or coincide with social responsibility development across childhood and adolescence.

Emotional Development. Empathy is an affective response to another person's situation (Hoffman, 2000). Becoming less ego-focused and more other-focused over time, empathy starts out as biased toward others who are proximal and similar to oneself and gradually expands to unfamiliar others and abstract individuals and groups (Eisenberg, Spinrad, & Sadovsky, 2006). Importantly, when moral principles are combined with activation of empathy, empathy-based arousal becomes less biased toward familiar others and extends more broadly to unfamiliar others (Hoffman, 2000). As empathy is an emotional foundation of caring for others, it may be the earliest developing precursor of social responsibility.

Empathy-related responding is associated with prosocial and altruistic behavior (Batson, Ahmad, & Stocks, 2004), yet personal distress in reaction to another's situation is not (Eisenberg, 2000). Thus, emotion regulation may also be an important developmental precursor for social responsibility. The link between emotion regulation and social responsibility is logical, as engaging in prosocial behavior often requires controlling one's own negative emotions while also helping others to regulate theirs. Empathy overarousal could lead to *less* concern for others, as overarousal can transfer into personal emotional distress (Hoffman, 2000). People with adaptive emotion regulation skills may be more likely to turn empathetic responding into addressing others' needs rather than turning feelings inward and reacting through personal distress. With emotion regulation skills in place, youth may be able to harness their passions in service of a social cause (see Hart, Atkins, & Fegley, 2003). Thus, empathy and emotion regulation may be key developmental foundations of social responsibility. However, given that values are part cognition and part emotion, emotions alone cannot explain social responsibility.

Cognitive Development. Executive functioning skills are theorized to be childhood precursors of social responsibility. Drawing from writing on civic engagement, three primary components of executive function may be useful for understanding social responsibility—inhibition, working memory, and cognitive flexibility (Astuto & Ruck, 2010). Executive function has been shown to enhance social behaviors and learning environments in childhood, which may promote prosocial behaviors and civic engagement.

Inhibition is the ability to forgo desires in favor of higher-order goals; for example, children may give money to help someone else instead of buying something for themselves. This cognitive skill relates to emotion regulation, as inhibition of one's own emotions allows individuals to consider the needs of others (Eisenberg, 2000). Working memory entails the ability to actively retain relevant information for reasoning, learning, and manipulation of complex concepts (Astuto & Ruck, 2010). The capacity for abstract thinking, necessary for conceptualizing values, typically develops during adolescence and relies on working memory. Thus, increasing information processing and abstract-thinking abilities deepen adolescents' capacities to adopt a socially responsible orientation. Cognitive flexibility is the ability to alter one's perspective and adapt to changing environmental demands (Astuto & Ruck, 2010). The related concept of perspective taking, which develops across childhood and adolescence, requires advanced cognitive processing, and can evoke empathetic arousal and enhance prosocial behaviors (Hoffman, 2000). Perspective taking also enables children and adolescents to consider the social contexts of moral decisions (Smetana & Villalobos, 2009). As social responsibility is inherently linked to interpersonal relationships, the ability to view the world from multiple vantage points enables young people to formulate personal obligations to exhibit care and justice.

More broadly, increases in sociocognitive capacities for reasoning about morality and responsibility have been documented across adolescence (Smetana & Villalobos, 2009). With age and maturity, prosocial reasoning recognizes that behaviors are intrinsically motivated by values and goals rather than based on external rewards (Mussen & Eisenberg, 2001). Similarly, compared to younger adolescents, older adolescents are more likely to say that moral values and social responsibility are the basis for their prosocial behaviors (Carlo, Eisenberg, & Knight, 1992). An understanding of rights and democratic decision making develops in middle childhood, and perhaps even earlier (Helwig, Arnold, Tan, & Boyd, 2007). Thus, a certain amalgam of cognitive skills set the stage for social responsibility. Programs and policies already designed to enhance executive function or moral reasoning may have positive benefits for the cultivation of social responsibility.

Self and Identity Development. Self and identity development are central to understanding social responsibility for at least two reasons. First, as noted, social responsibility is a value, and values unify personal identities (Hitlin, 2003). Therefore, social responsibility can offer insights into current and future selves. Second, social responsibility is fulfilling to the self (Peterson & Seligman, 2004). By implication, social responsibility is not solely altruistic, and approaches to social responsibility recognize that individuals can receive personal gains when contributing to the greater good.

Self-concept takes shape in childhood and precedes identity formation in adolescence (Côté, 2009); indeed, the ability to distinguish between self and others is a universal human cognition that starts developing very early in life (Hart & Fegley, 1997). Cross-cultural work suggests that societies socialize an emphasis on an interdependent or an independent self (Markus & Kitayama, 1991), concepts similar to the personal value orientations of self-transcendence versus self-enhancement (Schwartz, 1992). The way children and adolescents think about themselves in relation to others is important for social responsibility, which entails striking a balance between needs of self and others.

A key component of identity development is exploration (Erikson, 1968). Adolescence is characterized by exploring moral commitments, views about the world, and relationships with others (Flanagan, 2004). As adolescents "try on" identities to discover what gives them meaning in life, some may volunteer to help others, join a community group, or take up social causes. In fact, volunteering is increasingly common among adolescents, particularly among those from more privileged social classes, likely because they have more opportunities for civic engagement and identity exploration (Syvertsen, Wray-Lake, Flanagan, Osgood, & Briddell, 2011). A study of adolescents displaying exemplary care and community involvement illustrated that, compared with a matched sample, care exemplars endorsed more moral characteristics as part of the self and viewed their identity as more consistent and coherent (Hart & Fegley, 1995). Thus, social responsibility may arise out of processes of consolidating identities.

Seedbeds of Social Responsibility: Families, Peers, Schools, and Communities

Social responsibility germinates in the intimate relationships and settings that structure young people's daily lives. Some contexts do a better job than others of inculcating social responsibility by encouraging individuals to consider the implications of their actions on others and express concerns in self-transcendent ways. In these ways and others, families, peers, schools, and communities can create opportunities to socialize social responsibility in children and adolescents.

Ecological systems and social capital theories provide a strong theoretical basis for prioritizing the role of contexts in the development of social responsibility. An ecological systems perspective recognizes that development does not happen in a vacuum but rather in relationships, homes, schools, and neighborhoods (Bronfenbrenner & Morris, 2006). Young people's internal developmental capacities are bidirectionally associated with these proximal contexts; thus, fostering social responsibility requires focusing on children and adolescents' emotional, cognitive, and identity development *and* cultivating proximal contexts that prime social responsibility. Likewise, according to social capital theory, reciprocal social relationships set the stage for individuals to collectively resolve social problems, cultivate feelings of trust, and amplify awareness that actions have implications for others (Putnam, 2000). Social capital is not always inclusive, however. Bonding social capital (existing in close ties with immediate family, friends, and neighbors) is more likely than bridging social capital (characterizing more casual relationships) to reinforce exclusive identities and homogeneous groups (Putnam, 2000). From a developmental perspective, we posit that bonding social capital is normative during early and middle childhood when young people spend considerable time with family and have limited opportunities for sustained interactions with others. However, bridging social capital should become increasingly possible during adolescence as young people become more autonomous and have increased opportunities to interact with more diverse others. Although both forms of social capital have developmental benefits, bridging social capital may lay the foundation for social responsibility based on universalism rather than benevolence.

Mechanisms for Cultivating Social Responsibility. A review of research reveals that common mechanisms may operate to promote social responsibility across the proximal contexts of families, peers, schools, and communities. These mechanisms include modeling prosocial behaviors, communicating value socialization messages, and providing opportunities to practice socially responsible behaviors.

Modeling Prosocial Behaviors. In infancy and early childhood, parents are most often the reigning role models. As children enroll in school, become increasingly invested in friendships, and participate in community activities, the pool of potential role models widens beyond immediate and extended family to include peers, teachers, youth leaders, and other adults. Bridging social capital can take root in these relationships. In accordance with social learning theory (Bandura, 1977), the more opportunities young people have to witness others acting in socially responsible ways (e.g., recycling, standing up for a peer who is treated unfairly) and modeling emotions such as empathy, the more likely they are to mirror these actions (Eisenberg & Mussen, 1989). To the extent that modeled behaviors are repeated and perceived as resulting in favorable outcomes, they are more likely to be internalized in behavior and identity.

Drawing from the civic literature, we know that parent civic engagement is a strong predictor of youth civic engagement. For example, children whose parents regularly model civic engagement and democratic political discussion are more likely to be politically active (Verba, Burns, & Schlozman, 2003). The same type of behavioral modeling can occur in schools. When educators model democratic practices, by encouraging deliberative dialogue and creating an open classroom climate, students are more inclined to engage in civic activities and make informed decisions about which elected officials to support (Campbell, 2008; Torney-Purta, 2002), both expressions of social responsibility. To the extent that behavior communicates values, modeling can be considered one mechanism for socializing values of social responsibility; another mechanism is explicit communication of value messages.

Value Socialization Messages. Parents communicate explicit value messages to children in daily interactions (Grusec & Goodnow, 1994). Verbal communication is an important strategy for teaching values because parents may aspire to instill values that differ from the ones they hold for themselves or directly model. Given that socialization strategies may differ depending on the content of values being socialized (Grusec, Goodnow, &

Kuczynski, 2000), processes of socializing social responsibility may be unique from strategies to socialize other values such as self-enhancement.

Parents use various value socialization strategies to promote social responsibility, including communicating compassion and disciplinary messages. Direct efforts to socialize compassion and sensitize children to the needs of others have been positively associated with adolescents' social responsibility (Wray-Lake, 2010) as well as related constructs of moral reasoning (Pratt, Skoe, & Arnold, 2004) and social views about others (Flanagan & Tucker, 1999). Disciplinary encounters between parents and children also offer opportunities to communicate values and scaffold moral development (Grusec & Goodnow, 1994). When parents use inductive strategies to point out the victim's perspective during a disciplinary conversation, young people can more easily see connections between their behavior and harm to others (Hoffman, 2000). Teachers similarly encourage social responsibility when, for example, they admonish inappropriate (or, affirm appropriate) behavior by pointing out how a student's actions affect his or her classmates. As implied by these mechanisms, communicating compassion messages and using inductive reasoning may prompt young people to internalize social responsibility through the activation of empathetic concern.

Just as value messages can promote socially responsible values, so too can they erode them. For example, schools that heavily emphasize merit and competition among students often do so at the cost of promoting justice and caring (Hoffman, 2000). The role of value communication in cultivating social responsibility is important to study further because these messages are often implicitly embedded in cultural practices (e.g., expectations, pedagogical methods) rather than being formally taught.

Opportunities to Practice. Practice can help young people enhance perspective-taking abilities, spur further identity development, and build self-efficacy in the civic arena. Self-efficacy is particularly important as responsibility without agency rarely translates into action, thereby contributing little to the greater good (Youniss & Yates, 1997). Three contexts that provide rich opportunities to practice social responsibility are peer relationships, school and activity settings, and community service.

Outside of parent–child bonds, peers represent the first "others" with whom many young people form relationships. In friendships, young people learn how to balance interests of self and others as they work out what it means to care for others and maintain healthy relationships (Syvertsen & Flanagan, 2006). Unlike youth–adult relationships, peer relationships tend to be more egalitarian, making it both more necessary and more comfortable for young people to engage in perspective taking and conflict resolution. These skills can advance moral development (Eisenberg et al., 2006). Friendships are also important gateways to developing social responsibility through service activities (Syvertsen & Flanagan, 2006); having companionship and peer support in trying out new activities may motivate youth to encourage friends to participate in school and community activities.

Schools often operate like mini-polities where young people experience democratic participation and learn what it means to be a community member. Schools characterized by a climate of care and openness are ideal training grounds for learning and practicing important civic skills like articulating and defending political opinions and understanding the rights and responsibilities inherent in group membership. Many school- and community-based extracurricular activities also cultivate social responsibility by fostering a sense of social relatedness and encouraging teamwork whereby youth are expected (by peers and adult leaders, alike) to fulfill certain commitments to the group. Controlling for a host of other factors, participation in extracurricular activities during adolescence has been positively linked with both service to others and voting in young adulthood (Hart, Donnelly, Youniss, & Atkins, 2007). Thus, school and afterschool settings can enrich young people's democratic experiences, which in turn may foster growth in social responsibility.

Service to others—whether through service learning, an organization, or on one's own—is instrumental in cultivating social responsibility. In their in-depth case study of adolescents' service at a homeless shelter, Youniss and Yates (1997) detail the breadth of transformations young people can undergo when they lend their time, companionship, and skills to improving the lives of others. When paired with critical reflection, service can be a powerful mechanism for breaking down stereotypes about others, transcending one's own needs and social station, and developing other-oriented aspects of one's identity (Johnson, Beebe, Mortimer, & Snyder, 1998). Quasi-experimental studies comparing youth in service-learning programs with nonparticipating peers showed that participation in service positively predicted youth's social responsibility and future civic commitments (e.g., Scales, Blyth, Berkas, & Kielsmeier, 2000). Service provides a forum to display empathetic concern, refine cognitive abilities, and reflect on social issues, processes that develop a richer ethic of social responsibility.

Importantly, not all young people are afforded equal opportunities to engage in experiences that enable socialization and practice of social responsibility. Historical data show a persistent gap in political participation based on socioeconomic status (Verba et al., 2003), and some evidence suggests that the gap may be growing among youth (Syvertsen et al., 2011). The intergenerational transmission of class advantage in America makes it difficult for children of less educated and less civically engaged parents and those living in poor communities to access the adult role models, quality school programs, and community-based youth organizations important for social responsibility promotion (Verba et al., 2003). For example, service learning is not offered equally to all students, with the disadvantage shouldered by students not bound for college

(Kahne & Middaugh, 2008). It is incumbent on researchers, policy makers, community leaders, teachers, and other adults who actively work with youth to consider ways to rectify these inequalities so that more voices are represented in the democratic process.

Conclusions and Future Directions

Social responsibility is consolidated during adolescence when cognitive, emotional, and identity development converges with exposure to modeling, value messages, and opportunities for practice across contexts. Extant literature also suggests that a range of important precursors and early manifestations of social responsibility are already present in childhood. Very little of this work explicitly focused on social responsibility, but rather central themes were inferred from research on conceptually related constructs. Thus, longitudinal research on social responsibility is urgently needed that spans the first two decades of life and links key developmental constructs such as empathy, emotion regulation, executive function, and identity exploration to social responsibility and related civic actions.

Our review of the processes by which social responsibility is cultivated in childhood and adolescence across contexts suggests promising avenues for altering the developmental course of social responsibility. A single context is not paramount, but rather various settings such as family, peer, school, and community environments can plant the seeds of social responsibility through directly socializing social responsibility as well as indirectly cultivating cognitive and socioemotional competences. Experimental designs would offer rigorous tests of the role of contexts in increasing young people's social responsibility and related civic behaviors. Interventions designed to encourage social responsibility across contexts may benefit from focusing on mechanisms of modeling, value, and disciplinary messages, and providing opportunities to practice civic skills. Likewise, adults who work with youth can explicitly incorporate a social responsibility lens into interactions by, for example, fostering perspective taking by pointing out others' needs and feelings, encouraging service experiences and reflection, and respecting youths' opinions. Indeed, everyday relationships founded on trust, reciprocity, and democratic dialogue are likely to influence children and adolescents' developmental pathways toward social responsibility. Helping young people establish bridging social capital, through forming relationships with diverse others, for example, is also a potential avenue for enhancing social responsibility.

Given that some scholars argue that values are formed in adolescence yet crystallize in young adulthood (Jennings, 1989), putting resources toward the cultivation of social responsibility in childhood and adolescence seems like a worthwhile endeavor. Longitudinal investigations could also shed light on how stable social responsibility is once it is formed. Extant literature suggests that individuals do not simply choose their values nor are they entirely predestined (cf. Hitlin & Piliavin, 2004); rather, they take root based on developmental experiences and interactions with others. Social responsibility is likely constrained by some stable forces yet also has a component that is open to revision across the lifespan. In addition, we know little about how individuals come to define their "radius of others," but distinctions in social responsibility orientations have important implications for whether young citizens are empowered to help neighbors (benevolence), challenge power structures (universalism), or both.

Due to space limitations, we could not thoroughly delve into individual differences in social responsibility and its developmental precursors, yet heterogeneity may be evident by gender, ethnicity, and socioeconomic background. Most developmental research on social responsibility and related constructs has been conducted with middle class American youth. Future work should prioritize samples with more cultural diversity and international representation. It is also important to recognize that not all youth follow the same developmental pathways: contexts may affect youth differently depending on personal and background characteristics, or even genetic predispositions. Focusing on individual differences in *processes* based on personal characteristics and social group membership can help us understand the complexities in social responsibility development and give insights into how to intervene to address disparities in civic opportunities.

Given its rich developmental roots, social responsibility should garner more explicit attention from developmental scientists, civic scholars, and youth development workers. Social responsibility motivates a certain kind of citizenship that is rooted in care and justice and stems from obligations to contribute to society. These kinds of citizens are positive agents of democracy. Thus, it is important that we—as the shepherds of the next generation of citizens—be intentional about promoting social responsibility in children and adolescents by cultivating competencies across emotional, cognitive, and identity domains and enriching contexts that support rather than impede social responsibility development.

References

Astuto, J., & Ruck, M. D. (2010). Early childhood as a foundation for civic engagement. In L. R. Sherrod, J. Torney-Purta, C. A. Flanagan, L. R. Sherrod, J. Torney-Purta, & C. A. Flanagan (Eds.), *Handbook of research on civic engagement in youth* (pp. 249–275). Hoboken, NJ: Wiley.

Ballinger, J. (2006). United students against sweatshops. In L. Sherrod, C. A. Flanagan, R. Kassimir, & A. K. Syvertsen (Eds.), *Youth activism: An international encyclopedia* (pp. 663–667). Westport, CT: Greenwood Publishing.

Bandura, A. (1977). *Social learning theory*. Upper Saddle River, NJ: Prentice Hall.

Batson, C., Ahmad, N., & Stocks, E. L. (2004). Benefits and liabilities of empathy-induced altruism. In A. G. Miller (Ed.), *The social psychology of good and evil* (pp. 359–385). New York, NY: Guilford Press.

Baumeister, R. F., & Leary, M. R. (1995). The need to belong: Desire for interpersonal attachments as a fundamental human motivation. *Psychological Bulletin, 117*(3), 497–529. doi:10.1037/0033–2909.117.3.497

Berman, S. (1997). *Children's social consciousness and the development of social responsibility*. Albany, NY: State University of New York Press.

Bronfenbrenner, U., & Morris, P. A. (2006). The bioecological model of human development. In R. M. Lerner & W. Damon (Eds.), *Handbook of child psychology. Vol. 1. Theoretical models of human development* (6th ed., pp. 793–828). Hoboken, NJ: Wiley.

Campbell, D. E. (2008). Voice in the classroom: How an open classroom climate fosters political engagement among adolescents. *Political Behavior, 30*, 437–454. doi:10.1007/s11109–008–9063-z

Carlo, G., Eisenberg, N., & Knight, G. P. (1992). An objective measure of adolescents' prosocial moral reasoning. *Journal of Research on Adolescence, 2*(4), 331–349. doi:10.1207/s15327795jra0204_3

Côté, J. E. (2009). Identity formation and self-development in adolescence. In R. M. Lerner & L. Steinberg (Eds.), *Handbook of adolescent psychology. Vol. 1. Individual bases of adolescent development* (3rd ed., pp. 266–304). Hoboken, NJ: Wiley.

Eisenberg, N. (2000). Emotion, regulation, and moral development. *Annual Review of Psychology, 51*, 665–697. doi:10.1146/annurev.psych.51.1.665

Eisenberg, N., & Mussen, P. H. (1989). *The roots of prosocial behavior in children*. New York, NY: Cambridge University Press.

Eisenberg, N., Spinrad, T. L., & Sadovsky, A. (2006). Empathy-related responding in children. In M. Killen & J. G. Smetana (Eds.), *Handbook of moral development* (pp. 517–549). Mahwah, NJ: Erlbaum.

Erikson, E. H. (1968). *Identity: Youth and crisis*. New York, NY: W. W. Norton.

Flanagan, C. A. (2003). Trust, identity, and civic hope. *Applied Developmental Science, 7*, 165–171.

Flanagan, C. A. (2004). Volunteerism, leadership, political socialization, and civic engagement. In R. M. Lerner, & L. Steinberg, (Eds.), *Handbook of adolescent psychology* (2nd ed., pp. 721–745). Hoboken, NJ: Wiley.

Flanagan, C., Cumsille, P., Gill, S., & Gallay, L. (2007). School and community climates and civic commitments: Processes for ethnic minority and majority students. *Journal of Educational Psychology, 99*(2), 421–431. doi:10.1037/0022–0663.99.2.421

Flanagan, C. A., & Tucker, C. J. (1999). Adolescents' explanations for political issues: Concordance with their views of self and society. *Developmental Psychology, 35*, 1198–1209. doi:10.1037/0012–1649.35.5.1198

Gallay, L. (2006). Social responsibility. In L. Sherrod, C. A. Flanagan, R. Kassimir, & A. K. Syvertsen (Eds.), *Youth activism: An international encyclopedia* (pp. 599–602). Westport, CT: Greenwood Publishing.

Gilligan, C. (1982). New maps of development: New visions of maturity. *American Journal of Orthopsychiatry, 52*(2), 199–212.

Grusec, J. E., & Goodnow, J. J. (1994). Impact of parental discipline methods on the child's internalization of values: A reconceptualization of current points of view. *Developmental Psychology, 30*(1), 4–19. doi:10.1037/0012–1649.30.1.4

Grusec, J. E., Goodnow, J. J., & Kuczynski, L. (2000). New directions in analyses of parenting contributions to children's acquisition of values. *Child Development, 71*, 205–211.

Hart, D., Atkins, R., & Fegley, S. (2003). Personality and development in childhood: A person-centered approach. *Monographs of the Society for Research in Child Development, 68*(1), vii–109. doi:10.1111/1540–5834.00231

Hart, D., Donnelly, T. M., Youniss, J., & Atkins, R. (2007). High school community service as a predictor of adult voting and volunteering. *American Educational Research Journal, 44*, 197–219.

Hart, D., & Fegley, S. (1995). Prosocial behavior and caring in adolescence: Relations to self-understanding and social judgment. *Child Development*, 66(5), 1346–1359. doi:10.2307/1131651

Helwig, C. C., Arnold, M., Tan, D., & Boyd, D. (2007). Mainland Chinese and Canadian adolescents' judgments and reasoning about the fairness of democratic and other forms of government. *Cognitive Development*, 22(1), 96–109. doi:10.1016/j.cogdev.2006.07.002

Hitlin, S. (2003). Values as the core of personal identity: Drawing links between two theories of self. *Social Psychology Quarterly, 66*, 118–137. doi:10.2307/1519843

Hitlin, S., & Piliavin, J. A. (2004). Values: Reviving a dormant concept. *Annual Review of Sociology, 30*, 359–393.

Hoffman, M. L. (2000). *Empathy and moral development: Implications for caring and justice.* New York, NY: Cambridge University Press.

Jennings, M. K. (1989). The crystallization of orientations. In M.K. Jennings and J. van Deth (Eds.), *Continuities in political action* (pp. 313–348). Berlin, Germany: DeGruyter.

Johnson, M. K., Beebe, T., Mortimer, J. T., & Snyder, M. (1998). Volunteerism in adolescence: A process perspective. *Journal of Research on Adolescence, 8*, 309–332.

Kahne, J., & Middaugh, E. (2008, February). *Democracy for some: The civic opportunity gap in high school* (Working Paper 59). College Park, MD: CIRCLE.

Kohlberg, L. (1981). *Essays on moral development. Vol. I: The philosophy of moral development.* San Francisco, CA: Harper & Row.

Kohlberg, L., & Candee, D. (1984). The relationship of moral judgment to moral action. In L. Kohlberg (Ed.), *The psychology of moral development: The nature and validity of moral stages* (Vol. 2, pp. 498–581). San Francisco, CA: Harper & Row.

Markus, H. R., & Kitayama, S. (1991). Culture and the self: Implications for cognition, emotion, and motivation. *Psychological Review, 98*(2), 224–253. doi:10.1037/0033-295X.98.2.224

Mayton, D. M., II, & Furnham, A. (1994). Value underpinnings of antinuclear political activism: A cross-national study. *Journal of Social Issues, 50*, 117–128.

Mussen, P., & Eisenberg, N. (2001). Prosocial development in context. In A. C. Bohart & D. J. Stipek (Eds.), *Constructive & destructive behavior: Implications for family, school, & society* (pp. 103–126). Washington, DC: American Psychological Association. doi:10.1037/10433–005

Peterson, C., & Seligman, M. E. P. (2004). *Character strengths and virtues: A handbook and classification.* New York, NY: Oxford University Press.

Pratt, M. W., Hunsberger, B., Pancer, M., & Alisat, S. (2003). A longitudinal analysis of personal values socialization: Correlates of a moral self-ideal in late adolescence. *Social Development, 12*, 563–585.

Pratt, M. W., Skoe, E. E., & Arnold, M. (2004). Care reasoning development and family socialisation patterns in later adolescence: A longitudinal analysis. *International Journal of Behavioral Development, 28*(2), 139–147. doi:10.1080/01650250344000343

Putnam, R. D. (2000). *Bowling alone: The collapse and revival of American community.* New York, NY: Simon and Schuster.

Scales, P. C., Blyth, D. A., Berkas, T. H., & Kielsmeier, J. C. (2000). The effects of service-learning on middle school students' social responsibility and academic success. *The Journal of Early Adolescence, 20*, 332–358.

Schwartz, S. H. (1992). Universals in the content and structure of values: Theoretical advances and empirical tests in 20 countries. *Advances in Experimental Social Psychology, 25*, 1–65.

Smetana, J. G., & Villalobos, M. (2009). Social cognitive development in adolescence. In R. M. Lerner & L. Steinberg (Eds.), *Handbook of adolescent psychology. Vol. 1: Individual bases of adolescent development* (3rd ed., pp. 187–228). Hoboken, NJ: Wiley.

Syvertsen, A. K., & Flanagan, C. A. (2006). Peer influences on political development. In L. Sherrod, C. A. Flanagan, R. Kassimir, & A. K. Syvertsen (Eds.), *Youth activism: An international encyclopedia* (pp. 462–466). Westport, CT: Greenwood Publishing.

Syvertsen, A. K., Flanagan, C. A., & Stout, M. (2009). Code of silence: Students' perceptions of school climate and willingness to intervene in a peer's dangerous plan. *Journal of Educational Psychology, 101,* 219–232. doi:10.1037/a0013246

Syvertsen, A. K., Wray-Lake, L., Flanagan, C. A., Osgood, D. W., & Briddell, L. (2011). Thirty year trends in American adolescents' civic engagement: A story of changing participation and educational differences. *Journal of Research on Adolescence, 21*(3), 586–594. doi:10.1111/j.1532–7795.2010.00706.x

Torney-Purta, J. (2002). Patterns in the civic knowledge, engagement, and attitudes of European adolescents: The IEA Civic Education Study. *European Journal of Education, 37,* 129–141.

Verba, S., Burns, N., & Schlozman, K. (2003). Unequal at the starting line: Creating participatory inequalities across generations and among groups. *The American Sociologist, 34,* 45–69.

Verplanken, B., & Holland, R. W. (2002). Motivated decision making: Effects of activation and self-centrality of values on choices and behavior. *Journal of Personality and Social Psychology, 82,* 434–447.

Watts, R. J., & Flanagan, C. (2007). Pushing the envelope on youth civic engagement: A developmental and liberation psychology perspective. *Journal of Community Psychology, 35*(6), 779–792. doi:10.1002/jcop.20178

Westheimer, J., & Kahne, J. (2004). What kind of citizen? The politics of educating for democracy. *American Educational Research Journal, 41*(2), 237–269. doi:10.3102/00028312041002237

Wray-Lake, L. (2010). *The development of social responsibility in adolescence: Dynamic socialization, values, and action* (Unpublished doctoral dissertation). The Pennsylvania State University, University Park, PA.

Youniss, J., & Yates, M. (1997). *Community service and social responsibility in youth.* Chicago, IL: The University of Chicago Press.

Zaff, J., Boyd, M., Li, Y., Lerner, J. V., & Lerner, R. M. (2010). Active and engaged citizenship: Multi-group and longitudinal factorial analysis of an integrated construct of civic engagement. *Journal of Youth and Adolescence, 39*(7), 736–750. doi:10.1007/s10964–010–9541–6

LAURA WRAY-LAKE *is assistant professor of psychology at Claremont Graduate University. E-mail: laura.wray-lake@cgu.edu*

AMY K. SYVERTSEN *is a research scientist at Search Institute, Minneapolis, MN. E-mail: amys@search-institute.org*

3

Taking Stock of Youth Organizing: An Interdisciplinary Perspective

Brian D. Christens, Ben Kirshner

Abstract

Youth organizing combines elements of community organizing, with its emphasis on ordinary people working collectively to advance shared interests, and positive youth development, with its emphasis on asset-based approaches to working with young people. It is expanding from an innovative, but marginal approach to youth and community development into a more widely recognized model for practice among nonprofit organizations and foundations. Along the way, it has garnered attention from researchers interested in civic engagement, social movements, and resiliency. A growing body of published work evidences the increasing interest of researchers, who have applied an assortment of theoretical perspectives to their observations of youth organizing processes. Through an appraisal of the current state of this still-emerging area of practice and research, including case examples, the authors identify common elements of the practice of youth organizing—relationship development, popular education, social action, and participatory research and evaluation—and conclude with a discussion of promising future directions for research and practice. © 2011 Wiley Periodicals, Inc.

New Directions for Child and Adolescent Development, no. 134, Winter 2011 © Wiley Periodicals, Inc.
Published online in Wiley Online Library (wileyonlinelibrary.com). • DOI: 10.1002/cd.309

The Funder's Collaborative on Youth Organizing (2009) defines youth organizing as "an innovative youth development and social justice strategy that trains young people in community organizing and advocacy, and assists them in employing these skills to alter power relations and create meaningful institutional change in their communities." Like many forms of grassroots community organizing, youth organizing seeks to alter community conditions, but also has developmental impacts on participant-leaders. A definition that binds many forms of community organizing together is that they are "about activating people at a local, neighborhood level to claim power and make change for themselves" (Stoecker, 2009, pp. 21–22). Community organizing has traditionally been almost exclusively focused on adult participants. Youth organizing is primarily distinguished by the fact that it involves young people.[1]

In youth organizing initiatives, "the intent is to fight for rights and reform by addressing explicitly 'political' issues through direct action and advocacy" (Camino & Zeldin, 2002, p. 217). Issues addressed by youth organizing initiatives are typically local (e.g., school and neighborhood improvement), but the training and support of most youth organizing models situates these local struggles within broader political questions of resource distribution and racial and socioeconomic justice. An important distinction among youth organizing programs concerns whether the youth themselves select the issues, or whether issues are preselected by an organization. The latter is the case in many youth coalitions that use the term *youth organizing* for their activities. Our discussion herein relates solely to the more grassroots efforts in which youth organize around issues that they select themselves.

By many accounts, the practice of youth organizing is on the upswing. For example, a recent scan of the field of youth organizing (Torres-Fleming, Valdes, & Pillai, 2010) identified 160 youth organizing groups throughout the United States, in contrast to 120 such groups in 2004.[2] However, there is a great deal of turnover in the organizational settings for youth organizing. Many organizations that house youth organizing initiatives are small and have relatively short life cycles. A large proportion of the groups that were active in 2004 are no longer active. A number of the newer groups becoming active since 2004 are implementing intergenerational youth organizing (Hosang, 2006). The field of youth organizing, as a whole, is focused on community issues including (from most prevalent to least): education, racial justice, health, environmental justice, juvenile justice, immigrant rights, and issues related to gender and young women (Torres-Fleming et al., 2010). Many youth organizing initiatives are working to address multiple issues at one time. Other prominent issues addressed by youth organizing initiatives include reproductive justice; lesbian, gay, bisexual, transgender, and queer (LGBTQ) issues; Native American rights; and media representations of young people and minorities.

A confluence of factors has led to the increasing prevalence and traction of youth organizing during the past two decades. Perhaps most important, increasing levels of inequality over this period (Hacker & Pierson, 2010) have meant that working class people have struggled to maintain their quality of life. For instance, increasing educational inequality has fueled efforts by students and their allies to speak up for their rights to a quality education. These youth-driven efforts have paralleled an increasing focus on education among adult-led community organizing groups as well (Warren, Mira, & Nikundiwe, 2008). A second factor is the broader movement to include youth in civil society, including governance, citizenship, and organizations (Checkoway & Gutierrez, 2006; Christens & Zeldin, 2011). This movement has built steady and compounding influence within the academy, the foundation world, and in nonprofit organizations. It has emphasized youth as fully competent participants in society. Indeed, their exclusion from many settings has been framed as a social injustice (Delgado & Staples, 2008).

Although many community-organizing initiatives still exclude youth, community organizing, as a field, has been relatively quick to incorporate young people. In contrast, most government bodies and nonprofit organizations still fail to fully incorporate young people in their work. The greater flexibility of community organizing can perhaps be attributed to its tumultuous history, which has made it quite a nimble and adaptive field (Fisher, 1994). Organizing is also a field that is deeply concerned with injustice and exclusion. Hence, the growing understanding of age segregation as a form of injustice has found resonance. In addition, the history of community organizing has been characterized by pragmatic experimentation and cross-fertilization across formal and informal networks. In this context, it is easy to understand how some successful early adopters of youth organizing have relatively quickly influenced sibling groups, resulting in a rapid increase in multigenerational organizing campaigns.

Case Examples of Influential Youth Organizing Initiatives

To ground our discussion, we provide two examples of youth organizing initiatives that represent variation in how youth and adults work together. Both cases illustrate how youth organizing can be an effective strategy to positively impact social systems and participant leaders. The first case provides a demonstration of the power of youth organizing to alter the policies and settings that impact youth in their daily lives. The second case focuses on how youth organizing can have profound impacts on the development of the individuals involved.

Case #1: Institutional Impacts. Many youth organizing efforts have originated from within groups that were formerly involved exclusively in

NEW DIRECTIONS FOR CHILD AND ADOLESCENT DEVELOPMENT • DOI: 10.1002/cd

adult-focused community organizing. An example of such an effort is Contra Costa Interfaith Supporting Community Organization (CCISCO), a faith-based organizing initiative in Contra Costa County, California, that is affiliated with the PICO National Network.[3] Contra Costa County has a large population of young people, and many of the issues around which CCISCO adults have organized (such as immigration, health access, housing, and public safety) have had direct relevance to youth. Stahlhut (2003) details the organization's initial discussions around actually involving youth in the organizing process, beginning in 1999. As with many adult-oriented organizing initiatives, some adult leaders in CCISCO initially had reservations about youth involvement because of perceived differences in perspectives, life experiences, schedules, and interests. However, the group decided that one of their own organizing principles made a clear case for youth involvement in organizing, "the people closest to the problem should be involved in the solution to that problem" (p. 71). Based on this logic, CCISCO began a youth organizing initiative, and hired a diverse group of young people to organize their peers.

A decade later, CCISCO's experience is a demonstration of the power of youth organizing to impact local policies. For example, youth have organized successful campaigns to make the racial achievement gaps in local schools a policy priority. Results of this campaign have included policies that have led to a greater number of credentialed teachers and lower teacher turnover in schools with higher numbers of minority students. CCISCO youth also campaigned for, and won, an after-school youth center, and have taken action to improve the way that schools have tracked students for English as a Second Language classes (Speer, 2008).

Organizing younger people required some adaptations to the organizing model that CCISCO employs with adults. For instance, the local organizing committees that make up the larger organization had previously been exclusively faith-based institutions (e.g., congregations, parishes). Youth formed local organizing committees through faith-based institutions, but also through schools or other settings (e.g., community centers, neighborhoods). Meetings were planned differently. For example, meetings involved icebreakers and other interactive activities instead of more formal introductions (Stahlhut, 2003). Relationship development happened differently. For instance, instead of the one-to-one meetings that are a cornerstone of adult relational organizing (Christens, 2010), students collected surveys of their peers on community issues, initiating conversations that often led to more regular communication (Speer, 2008). In addition, CCISCO's youth trainings were geared specifically to a younger group of leaders. However, the basic goals and processes of community organizing have remained the same—building a powerful network of volunteer leaders to make community-level change. The early successes of CCISCO's youth organizing have influenced other local organizations in the PICO National Network and other networks that support local organizing.

Case #2: Youth Sociopolitical Development. In addition to community-level impacts described above, youth organizing offers a powerful context for individual development. Consider the case of the Social Justice Education Project (SJEP) in Tucson, Arizona. Unlike many organizing groups that are rooted in community organizations, SJEP is a university-school collaboration, which began in 2003 in the Tucson public schools (Cammarota, 2007; Cammarota & Romero, 2009). We view it as a case of organizing because of its emphasis on young people learning to critically interrogate their surroundings, identify shared experiences, and work together to advance social justice in their schools and communities.

The SJEP is a two-year curriculum for eleventh and twelfth graders, most of whom are Mexican American and Chicano, which draws on Freirean pedagogy (Freire, 1970) and critical race theory to engage students in critical reflection on American history and their educational experiences. In the junior year, the course meets state standards in American History and Government; in the senior year students develop social activism projects based on a youth participatory action research (YPAR) model. In YPAR, students reflect on their experiences; do ethnographic research to gain new insight; and drawing on research products, advocate for changes in their schools. For example, in SJEP's first year, students brought to light the segregation that existed between the main campus of Cerro High School and a newly built "law magnet school," which was a school within the larger campus. Students used a social mapping methodology to show that the law magnet mostly enrolled White students from middle-class neighborhoods, while there were a greater proportion of poor and low-income Mexican American students in the regular school. Students also created and showed a video that contrasted the advanced learning opportunities and technology in the law magnet (such as advanced placement [AP] classes, new computers, and elective law courses) with deteriorating facilities in the regular school. Cammarota (2008) reports that although audience members, including teachers and administrators, displayed mixed reactions to the video, the most egregious physical problems were addressed, such as dangerous machinery in the regular school's special education classroom. Since that first year, students have developed projects focused on improving a range of issues, including media representations of youth, cultural assimilation for Latino youth, and improved opportunities for active learning.

Research on learning and development in SJEP has focused on qualitative, youth-reported descriptions of changes in their learning (see Cammarota, 2007; Cammarota & Romero, 2009). These accounts suggest that participants develop sociopolitically, both in terms of shifts in their understanding of school and society and shifts in their sense of agency. For example, students describe a shift from being alienated or disconnected from school toward a deep engagement in learning, which stems from a new recognition of its relevance to their lives. One student, Validia, described the value of "learning about real stuff": "Learning is important . . . especially learning about real stuff. Like seeing the realities, how you are blinded by society. This, you know, you are able to see how dropping out of school, how not paying attention, you know, is just you becoming part of the system. This way, you know, it makes you want to work harder. Because you understand. You realize what is going on, and what, you know, what things are making you do this. So you go against it."

In addition to gaining greater insight about the context of their own lives, students report learning how to use academic tools—such as ethnography or critical theory—to interpret and challenge discrimination or inequality. Students begin to see academic content as a vehicle for them to accomplish their own goals. As Kati succinctly put it: "You have to learn how they talk, but say your story" (Cammarota, 2007, p. 93). Kati's comment suggests that she recognized the importance of gaining fluency in an academic discourse ("how they talk"), but as a vehicle for self-expression and empowerment ("say your story").

Common Elements of the Practice of Youth Organizing

Despite the diversity of practices in youth organizing, most models incorporate some version of the following elements: relationship development, popular education, social action, and research and evaluation.

Relationship Development. Organizing involves developing a constituency that can mobilize for community change around a common issue. This kind of social power is built through a network of trusting relationships. When these relationships are developed in an organizing context, they are known as *public relationships* (Christens, 2010). Relationship development processes in youth organizing tend to differ from those in adult organizing (Speer, 2008). For example, one-to-one meetings, often used in adult organizing, are rarely part of youth organizing processes. Instead, youth organizers use peer-administered surveys, icebreakers, group check-in conversations, games, activities, and unstructured social time to build relationships and uncover issues in young people's lives. Nevertheless, relationships are intentionally developed, and the functions are the same—to build commonalities and understandings of common issues, and to develop a network of trust and concern. Many have also noted youth organizing as a context that facilitates the development of supportive, working relationships across generations, including formal and informal mentoring (Christens & Zeldin, 2011; Kirshner, 2008; Share & Stacks, 2007).

Popular Education. By popular education, we mean not only the techniques that draw explicitly on the work of Paulo Freire (1970; see Watts, Diemer & Voight, this volume), but also the broader set of activities that build critical perspectives on social systems and the perpetuation of inequalities. Many youth organizing initiatives predominately involve

African Americans or Latinos. Indeed, many youth organizing groups have an explicit focus on racial justice, and primarily reach out to youth of color. In these initiatives, for instance, popular education often addresses racial disparities in education or health, immigrant rights, the prison-industrial complex, and the role of culture and racial identity in resistance (Ginwright, 2007). Other youth organizing initiatives are demographically diverse and may focus their educational efforts on building trust and solidarity across lines of race, class, ethnicity, or sexual identity (Russell, Muraco, Subramaniam, & Laub, 2009; Watkins, Larson, & Sullivan, 2007).

Social Action. Youth organizing builds leaders through relationship development and popular education, but it does not stop there. Young people then take action to alter power relationships in the communities where they live. These actions often involve hundreds, or even thousands of people. They are typically meticulously planned and choreographed with the goal of achieving policy or other systems change. In many models of youth social action, decision makers are invited to attend public actions and are asked to make commitments to specific decisions on issues (e.g., votes on bills in the city council, school or police policies, funding allocations). Local media are frequently invited. Reporting can both raise public awareness of the issue at hand and reinforce the power and competence of youth in the eyes of the public. In some cases, public actions are less specific in their policy goals and are more expressive and fluid, as in hip-hop or other arts-based forms of activism, which can both build group solidarity and raise public consciousness.

Participatory Research and Evaluation. In many models of youth organizing, large social actions are bracketed by research and evaluation. In one organizing initiative in San Bernardino, California (see Christens & Dolan, 2011), youth leaders partnered with local universities to conduct and analyze surveys of thousands of their peers to understand local youth violence and suggest solutions. These young organizers also thoroughly evaluate their own performances in meetings, offering constructive feedback to one another. Participants describe evaluation as key to their own leadership development. Youth in organizing learn research skills through a variety of activities that are situated within the overarching goal of community-level change. These activities include interviewing, designing surveys and collecting data, data analysis, policy and program research, and public presentations of research findings. Because these research skills are connected to the goal of change on issues that youth themselves have selected, they are more likely to be remembered and represent a powerful model for experiential learning (Kirshner & Geil, 2010). In these contexts, high-level academic skills and concepts are employed as tools to accomplish socially relevant ends. For example, Rogers, Morrell, and Enyedy (2007) reported that teen participants in UCLA's Institute for Democracy, Equality, and Access developed advanced academic skills, including reading sociology texts, analyzing oral histories, and designing surveys. These skills were deployed to learn about educational equity in Los Angeles and generate proposals for change. Rogers et al. quote one young alumnus of the institute who returned to talk to a later cohort: "During high school I didn't know if I was going to end up 6 feet under or if I was going to end up not graduating or just working or whatever. But through this research and through doing research and educating myself about what goes on in high schools . . . that research opened my eyes and presented me with *tools to create change* [italics added] and now I am dedicating my life to creating change" (p. 421).

Putting the Elements Together

Given the powerful combination of these elements, it should not be surprising that people are taking notice of youth organizing! Scholars of applied human development (Camino & Zeldin, 2002; Zeldin, Petrokubi & Camino, 2008), social work (Checkoway & Gutierrez, 2006; Delgado & Staples, 2008), education (Ginwright, 2010; Kirshner, 2009), sociology (Warren, Mira, & Nikundiwe, 2008), community health (Peterson, Dolan, & Hanft, 2010), and psychology (Christens & Dolan, 2011; Watts & Flanagan, 2007) have published recent studies of youth organizing efforts. In addition, foundations and intermediary groups have taken notice, resulting in a proliferation of publications on the practice (e.g., Fletcher & Vavrus, 2006) and impacts of youth organizing. The Funders' Collaborative on Youth Organizing, for example, has published eleven papers chronicling youth organizing theory and specific campaigns (http://www.fcyo .org/toolsandresources). Also, program evaluations, although not published in academic journals, have contributed useful information about the types of youth who join youth organizing groups and outcomes associated with their participation (e.g., Lewis-Charp, Cao Yu, Soukamneuth, & Lacoe, 2003; Mediratta et al., 2008).

Although scholars interested in youth organizing have different roles and disciplinary backgrounds, their interest in similar concepts draws them to youth organizing. Much of the attention from the research and foundation worlds is from people and groups interested in the promotion of social justice. Many are interested in holistic approaches to improving conditions (e.g., housing, community development) and outcomes (e.g., educational outcomes, crime statistics) in low-income communities. Many are interested in civic engagement, and some are hoping to support the development of social movements. Finally, many are interested in community processes that support youth development, including the development of strategic thinking, civic habits, and critical understandings of the social and political spheres. Because youth organizing is a transactional process that trains and supports young leaders to alter power relations and improve community conditions, these diverse interests have all provided interesting perspectives on youth organizing processes and outcomes.

NEW DIRECTIONS FOR CHILD AND ADOLESCENT DEVELOPMENT • DOI: 10.1002/cd

For scholars of applied human development, organizing represents a model or a promising pathway for the inclusion of young people as full participants in civil society (Camino & Zeldin, 2002). Youth organizing is also viewed as a context in which natural mentoring between generations, or youth–adult partnerships take place (Share & Stacks, 2007; Zeldin, Petrokubi, & Camino, 2008). These are viewed as crucial supports to the positive developmental outcomes of adolescence and emerging adulthood. Scholars of education have shown that involving young people in organizing increases their motivation to succeed in school (Mediratta et al., 2008). Community health researchers have found pathways from social capital—which is built through organizing—to health outcomes (Laser & Leibowitz, 2009). Additionally, many organizing initiatives directly seek to improve community health outcomes. For example, Peterson, Dolan, and Hanft (2010) describe a youth organizing initiative to reduce youth violence. In short, because youth organizing has attracted attention from numerous academic disciplines and foundations, an array of terms has been used to describe the process and outcomes. These include civic identity development, empowerment, civic engagement, social capital, sense of community, collective efficacy, social/experiential learning, sociopolitical development, radical healing, and social responsibility. This multidisciplinarity is what led us to develop a framework that locates these processes and outcomes at multiple levels of analysis.

A Multilevel Framework of Youth Organizing Processes and Outcomes

Examining the extant research on youth organizing, one feature comes into focus: youth organizing is a process that has impacts at multiple levels of analysis. In fact, youth organizing can be considered a community-based culturally relevant multilevel intervention—a category of interventions that Trickett (2009) identifies as "those that integrate a multi-layered ecological conception of the community context, a commitment to working in collaboration or partnership with groups and settings in the local community, and an appreciation of how intervention efforts are situated in local culture and context" (p. 257). In other words, because youth organizing involves local youth in culturally relevant efforts directed toward positive social change on issues they themselves select, the process can have positive developmental impacts on people (youth and adults) and communities. Moreover, as Tolman and colleagues (2001) point out, youth organizing initiatives are among the most effective settings for youth development and community development to occur simultaneously.

Youth organizing takes place through community-based organizations, which act as settings for youth development. However, the outcomes of youth organizing include impacts that are larger than these organizations when organizing initiatives are successful in changing local

Figure 1. Integrative Framework of Youth Organizing Processes and Outcomes

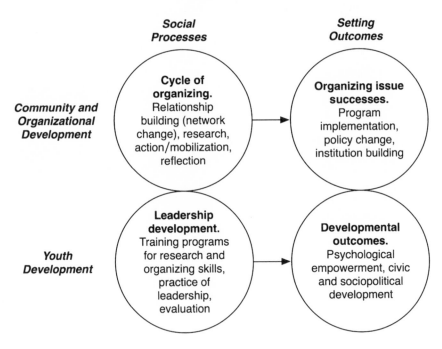

policies, implementing new programs, and building powerful political coalitions. Figure 1 provides a framework for understanding the processes and impacts of youth organizing at multiple levels of analysis. In the vertical dimension, we draw on Bronfenbrenner's (1977) ecological framework, which conceptualizes human development as occurring within multilayered contexts. In successful youth organizing initiatives, youth development and community/organizational development occur simultaneously through the same set of social processes. In the horizontal dimension, we draw on Tseng and Seidman's (2007) framework for setting-level change— particularly their distinction between social processes and setting outcomes. Social processes, defined as "interactions between people and their immediate environments" (Tseng & Seidman, 2007, p. 219), in youth organizing include peer and youth–adult partnerships, participatory research, leadership development, mobilization, and evaluation. Setting outcomes are defined by Tseng and Seidman (2007) as "how well the setting is functioning at a particular point in time" (p. 218); these include the ability of youth organizing initiatives to alter local policy, implement programs, and build powerful organizations.

Notably, setting outcomes also include developmental outcomes for youth, such as psychological empowerment and civic and sociopolitical development. Although it may seem counterintuitive to describe youth development as setting-level outcomes, we follow Tseng and Seidman's (2007) understanding of developmental outcomes at the level of settings to emphasize that it is the reciprocal transactions (Altman & Rogoff, 1987) occurring between youth organizing settings and individual youth that are producing these positive developmental outcomes. Finally, although not depicted in Figure 1, youth organizing has been identified as a driver of broader social change because it demonstrates the capacities and potential contributions of young people to the larger public (Christens & Dolan, 2011). Altering the public's view of youth leads to greater civic inclusion of young people—a critical contribution to the future of democracy.

Locating the Cutting Edge in Practice and Research

To conclude this interdisciplinary discussion of youth organizing, we seek to identify areas of emerging interest or underdevelopment in the literature. One of the lesser-told stories about youth organizing is the common use of "popular research," often called YPAR, as a vehicle for social action campaigns. There is typically a phase in organizing campaigns when youth participants gather data about a topic, such as surveying fellow students about their experiences in a school, mapping availability of fresh produce in a neighborhood, or performing content analyses of newspaper stories (Kirshner & Geil, 2010). In some cases, this research element may arise because of a direct collaboration with a university, as in the SJEP case described above. Nevertheless, groups also often carry out popular research independently of university collaborations (Warren, Mapp, & Community Organizing and School Reform Project, 2011). Such research is used both to help organizers better understand the issue and as evidence to share with policymakers or other stakeholders. It involves complex cognitive tasks, including developing survey items and analyzing qualitative data. Sometimes participants encounter data that may not adhere to the story they hoped to tell, which challenges participants to learn how to manage their biases (Kirshner, Pozzoboni, & Jones, 2011).

The kinds of learning opportunities that arise when participatory research is linked with social action campaigns merit further attention from researchers. For example, what kinds of local funds of knowledge (Moll, Amanti, Neff, & Gonzalez, 1992) do youth organizers draw on to collect or make sense of data? How do young people learn sophisticated research skills and in what ways does that process differ from their typical experiences with academic learning in schools? Attention to these questions can help the field better understand developmental outcomes in youth organizing and also may have implications for innovative approaches to schooling.

Following our framework depicting social processes and social outcomes, more research is needed on the ways that youth organizing

NEW DIRECTIONS FOR CHILD AND ADOLESCENT DEVELOPMENT • DOI: 10.1002/cd

initiatives function as developmental settings, particularly for disadvantaged or marginalized youth. To date, research has primarily been focused on descriptions of processes and associated developmental outcomes. The time is now ripe for studies of youth organizing that employ quantitative, quasi-experimental methods to compare youth organizing initiatives with each other, and with other settings that facilitate positive youth development. On the process side, promising methods include measuring and understanding patterns and forms of participation and engagement (Christens & Speer, 2011) and longitudinal analyses of social networks (Speer, 2008). Outcomes should also be measured at multiple levels of analysis. A perpetual difficulty in research on community organizing is demonstrating causal linkages between organizing initiatives and community-level outcomes. Developmental achievements of youth in organizing—including youth empowerment and civic and sociopolitical development—represent both important outcomes in themselves, as well as proximal outcomes (Javdani & Allen, 2011) for more distal community-level changes.

Finally, a vital point to note is that youth organizing is not universally appreciated. Organizing for community-level change inevitably creates conflict (Alinsky, 1971), and many of the targets of youth organizing initiatives have retaliated by seeking to stop youth organizing from occurring, or attacking its legitimacy. For example, in 2010 the Arizona Superintendent for Public Instruction sought to bar the Social Justice Education Project (described earlier in this chapter), and the broader ethnic studies program in Tucson from its work, claiming that it promoted un-American values (Zehr, 2010). Many youth organizers have described confrontations with authority figures in which the authorities have questioned the capabilities of young leaders, or sought to punish them for their organizing activities (Christens & Dolan, 2011). Research on youth organizing—particularly on the positive impacts on youth development—can bolster initiatives against such reactionary delegitimizing attempts by those who seek to maintain an authoritarian status quo in the settings that youth inhabit. More work is needed by researchers, including youth and their adult allies, to prepare the ground for youth organizers, by getting the word out about positive youth development and community development in these settings.

References

Alinsky, S. D. (1971). *Rules for radicals: A pragmatic primer for realistic radicals.* New York, NY: Vintage.

Altman, I., & Rogoff, B. (1987). World views in psychology: Trait, interactional, organismic, and transactional perspectives. In D. Stokols & I. Altman (Eds.), *Handbook of environmental psychology* (pp. 7–40). New York, NY: Wiley.

Bronfenbrenner, U. (1977). Toward an experimental ecology of human development. *American Psychologist, 32*(7), 513–531. doi:10.1037/0003–066X.32.7.513

Camino, L., & Zeldin, S. (2002). From periphery to center: Pathways for youth civic engagement in the day-to-day life of communities. *Applied Developmental Science*, 6(4), 213–220. doi:10.1207/S1532480XADS0604_8

Cammarota, J. (2007). A social justice approach to achievement: Guiding Latina/o students toward educational attainment with a challenging, socially relevant curriculum. *Equity and Excellence in Education*, 40, 87–96. doi:10.1080/10665680601015153

Cammarota, J. (2008). The cultural organizing of youth ethnographers: Formalizing a praxis-based pedagogy. *Anthropology & Education Quarterly*, 39(1), 45–58. doi:10.1111/j.1548-1492.2008.00004.x

Cammarota, J., & Romero, A. F. (2009). A social justice epistemology and pedagogy for Latina/o students: Transforming public education with participatory action research. In T. M. Brown & L. F. Rodriguez (Eds.), Youth in participatory action research. *New Directions for Youth Development*, 123, 53–65. doi:10.1002/yd.314

Checkoway, B. N., & Gutierrez, L. (2006). Youth participation and community change. *Journal of Community Practice*, 14(1), 1–9. doi:10.1300/J125v14n01_01

Christens, B. D. (2010). Public relationship building in grassroots community organizing: Relational intervention for individual and systems change. *Journal of Community Psychology*, 38(7), 886–900. doi:10.1002/jcop.20403

Christens, B. D., & Dolan, T. (2011). Interweaving youth development, community development, and social change through youth organizing. *Youth & Society*, 43(2), 528–548. doi:10.1177/0044118X10383647

Christens, B. D., & Speer, P. W. (2011). Contextual influences on participation in community organizing: A multilevel longitudinal study. *American Journal of Community Psychology*, 47(3–4), 253–263. doi:10.1007/s10464–010–9393-y

Christens, B. D., & Zeldin, S. (2011). Community engagement. In R. J. R. Levesque (Ed.), *Encyclopedia of adolescence*. New York, NY: Springer.

Delgado, M., & Staples, L. (2008). *Youth-led community organizing: Theory and action.* New York, NY: Oxford University Press.

Fisher, R. (1994). *Let the people decide: Neighborhood organizing in America* (Updated ed.). Boston, MA: Twayne.

Fletcher, A., & Vavrus, J. (2006). *The guide to social change led by and with young people.* Olympia, WA: CommonAction.

Freire, P. (1970). *Pedagogy of the oppressed.* New York, NY: Continuum.

Funders' Collaborative on Youth Organizing. (2009). *What is youth organizing?* Retrieved from http://www.fcyo.org/whatisyouthorganizing.

Ginwright, S. A. (2007). Black youth activism and the role of critical social capital in Black community organizations. *American Behavioral Scientist*, 51(3), 403–418. doi:10.1177/0002764207306068

Ginwright, S. A. (2010). Peace out to revolution! Activism among African American youth: An argument for radical healing. *Young*, 18(1), 77–96. doi:10.1177/1103308809901800106

Hacker, J. S., & Pierson, P. (2010). Winner-take-all politics: Public policy, political organization, and the precipitous rise of top incomes in the United States. *Politics & Society*, 38(2), 152–204. doi:10.1177/0032329210365042

Hosang, D. W. (2006). Family and community as the cornerstone of civic engagement: Immigrant and youth organizing in the southwest. *National Civic Review*, 95(4), 58–61. doi:10.1002/ncr.160

Javdani, S., & Allen, N. E. (2011). Proximal outcomes matter: A multilevel examination of the processes by which coordinating councils produce change. *American Journal of Community Psychology*, 47, 12–27. doi:10.1007/s10464–010–9375–0

Kirshner, B. (2008). Guided participation in three youth activism organizations: Facilitation, apprenticeship, and joint work. *Journal of the Learning Sciences*, 17(1), 60–101. doi:10.1080/10508400701793190

Kirshner, B. (2009). Power in numbers: Youth organizing as a context for exploring civic identity. *Journal of Research on Adolescence, 19*(3), 414–440. doi:10.1111/j.1532–7795.2009.00601.x

Kirshner, B., & Geil, K. (2010). "I'm about to bring it!" Access points between youth activists and adult policymakers. *Children, Youth Environments, 20*(2). Retrieved from http://www.colorado.edu/journals/cye/.

Kirshner, B., Pozzoboni, K., & Jones, H. (2011). Cognitive development outside of school: Learning to manage bias in participatory action research. *Applied Developmental Science, 15*(3), 140–155. doi:10.1080110665680601015153

Laser, J. A., & Leibowitz, G. S. (2009). Promoting positive outcomes for healthy youth development: Utilizing social capital theory. *Journal of Sociology and Social Welfare, 36*(1), 87–102.

Lewis-Charp, H., Cao Yu, H., Soukamneuth, S., & Lacoe, J. (2003). Extending the reach of youth development through civic activism: Outcomes of the Youth Leadership for Development Initiative. Oakland, CA: Social Policy Research Associates.

Mediratta, K., Shah, S., McAlister, S., Fruchter, N., Mokhtar, C., & Lockwood, D. (2008). Organized communities, stronger schools: A preview of research findings. Providence, RI: Annenberg Institute for School Reform at Brown University.

Moll, L. C., Amanti, C., Neff, D., & Gonzalez, N. (1992). Funds of knowledge for teaching: Using a qualitative approach to connect homes and classrooms. *Theory Into Practice, 31*(2), 132–141.

Peterson, T. H., Dolan, T., & Hanft, S. (2010). Partnering with youth organizers to prevent violence: An analysis of relationships, power, and change. *Progress in Community Health Partnerships: Research, Education, and Action, 4*(3), 235–242. doi:10.1353/cpr.2010.0011

Rogers, J., Morrell, E., & Enyedy, N. (2007). Studying the struggle: Contexts for learning and identity development for urban youth. *American Behavioral Scientist, 51*(3), 419–443. doi:10.1177/0002764207306069

Russell, S. T., Muraco, A., Subramaniam, A., & Laub, C. (2009). Youth empowerment and high school gay-straight alliances. *Journal of Youth and Adolescence, 38*(7), 891–903. doi:10.1007/s10964–008–9382–8

Share, R. A., & Stacks, J. S. (2007). Youth-adult partnership in community organizing: A case study of the My Voice Counts! campaign. *Journal of Community Practice, 14*(4), 113–127. doi:10.1300/J125v14n04_07

Speer, P. W. (2008). Altering patterns of relationship and participation: Youth organizing as a setting-level intervention. In M. Shinn & H. Yoshikawa (Eds.), *Toward positive youth development: Transforming schools and community programs* (pp. 213–228). New York, NY: Oxford University Press.

Stahlhut, D. (2003). The people closest to the problem. *Social Policy, 34*(2/3), 71–74.

Stoecker, R. (2009). Community organizing and social change. *Contexts, 8*(1), 20–25.

Tolman, J., Pittman, K., Cervonne, B., Cushman, K., Duque, S., Kinkaid, S., et al. (2001). *Youth acts, community impacts: Stories of youth engagement with real results*. Takoma Park, MD: The Forum for Youth Investment, International Youth Foundation.

Torres-Fleming, A., Valdes, P., & Pillai, S. (2010). *2010 field scan*. Brooklyn, NY: Funders' Collaborative on Youth Organizing.

Trickett, E. J. (2009). Multilevel community-based culturally situated interventions and community impact: An ecological perspective. *American Journal of Community Psychology, 43*, 257–266. doi:10.1007/s10464–009–9227–y

Tseng, V., & Seidman, E. (2007). A systems framework for understanding social settings. *American Journal of Community Psychology, 39*, 217–228. doi:10.1007/s10464–007–9101–8

Warren, M. R., Mapp, K. L., & Community Organizing and School Reform Project. (2011). *A match on dry grass: Community organizing as a catalyst for school reform*. New York, NY: Oxford University Press.

Warren, M. R., Mira, M., & Nikundiwe, T. (2008). Youth organizing: From youth development to school reform. In S. Deschenes, M. McLaughlin, & A. Newman (Eds.), Community organizing and youth advocacy. *New Directions for Youth Development, 117,* 27–42. doi:10.1002/yd.245

Watkins, N. D., Larson, R. W., & Sullivan, P. J. (2007). Bridging intergroup difference in a community youth program. *American Behavioral Scientist, 51*(3), 380–402. doi:10.1177/0002764207306066

Watts, R. J., Diemer, M. A., & Voight, A. M. (2011). Critical consciousness: Current status and future directions. In C. A. Flanagan, & B. D. Christens (Eds.), Youth civic development: Work at the cutting edge. *New Directions for Child & Adolescent Development, 134,* 43–57.

Watts, R. J., & Flanagan, C. (2007). Pushing the envelope on youth civic engagement: A developmental and liberation psychology perspective. *Journal of Community Psychology, 35*(6), 779–792. doi:10.1002/jcop.20178

Zehr, M. A. (2010, August 11). Arizona, Tucson at odds over ethnic studies. *Education Week.* Retrieved from http://www.edweek.org/ew/articles/2010/08/11/37arizona_ep.h29.html?qs = Zehr+Arizona.

Zeldin, S., Petrokubi, J., & Camino, L. (2008). *Youth-adult partnerships in public action: Principles, organizational culture and outcomes.* Washington, DC: Forum for Youth Investment.

Notes

1. Youth organizing initiatives are most often focused on high school aged students, but sometimes also involve college students and younger teens.

2. Although all of these groups involve some youth leadership, some of the groups in this field scan may not meet our definition of grassroots youth organizing for this chapter.

3. PICO stands for People Improving Communities through Organizing (http://www.piconetwork.org/).

BRIAN D. CHRISTENS *is assistant professor of human ecology at the University of Wisconsin–Madison. E-mail: bchristens@wisc.edu*

BEN KIRSHNER *is assistant professor of education at the University of Colorado, Boulder. E-mail: ben.kirshner@colorado.edu*

NEW DIRECTIONS FOR CHILD AND ADOLESCENT DEVELOPMENT • DOI: 10.1002/cd

4

Critical Consciousness: Current Status and Future Directions

Roderick J. Watts, Matthew A. Diemer, Adam M. Voight

Abstract

In this chapter, the authors consider Paulo Freire's construct of critical consciousness (CC) and why it deserves more attention in research and discourse on youth political and civic development. His approach to education and similar ideas by other scholars of liberation aims to foster a critical analysis of society—and one's status within it—using egalitarian, empowering, and interactive methods. The aim is social change as well as learning, which makes these ideas especially relevant to the structural injustice faced by marginalized youth. From their review of these ideas, the authors derive three core CC components: critical reflection, political efficacy, and critical action. They highlight promising research related to these constructs and innovative applied work including youth action-research methodology. Their conclusion offers ideas for closing some of the critical gaps in CC theory and research. © 2011 Wiley Periodicals, Inc.

NEW DIRECTIONS FOR CHILD AND ADOLESCENT DEVELOPMENT, no. 134, Winter 2011 © Wiley Periodicals, Inc.
Published online in Wiley Online Library (wileyonlinelibrary.com). • DOI: 10.1002/cd.310

For most scholars in the United States, youth social action aimed at the roots of social injustice is near the periphery of theory and research on civic engagement. In this chapter, we consider reasons why political development ought to be more central to the discourse. We make a case for this shift by describing the potential Freire's notion of "critical consciousness" has for informing youth development and activism. Critical consciousness (CC) describes how oppressed or marginalized people learn to critically analyze their social conditions and act to change them. Freire used it to increase literacy among Brazilian peasants, but he also used CC as a tool for liberation—helping those he worked with to "read the world" as they learned to "read the word" and then act on their world in the interest of justice. Our view is that youth civic education and engagement in the United States, especially for marginalized youth, can help them to understand themselves in a sociopolitical context as it did for the disenfranchised of Brazil. In addition to humanitarian activities and greater participation in electoral activities, marginalized youth would benefit from a social analysis that helps them understand and then resist unjust conditions through constructive social action. Although privileged youth have many more opportunities than those who are marginalized, they too can benefit from learning how social injustice operates and ways they can promote a more just society.

Although they are in the minority, there are scholars who recognize political activism as part of youth civic engagement. Westheimer and Kahne (2003) include it as one of their three forms of citizenship: (1) the personally responsible citizen who demonstrates citizenship through individual acts such as volunteering; (2) the participatory citizen who engages in local community affairs and stays current on local and national issues; and (3) the justice-oriented citizen who, like the participatory citizen, emphasizes collective work toward community betterment while maintaining a more "critical stance" on social, political, and economic issues. Like Freire, Westheimer and Kahne use the term "critical" to distinguish this justice-oriented perspective, but it is not a feature of the first two forms of citizenship. The participatory citizen stays "current" on social issues, but a critical reflection on the root causes of social conditions is not a priority. In contrast, the justice-oriented citizen is oriented toward collective action and structural perspectives on community betterment. In this chapter, we call it a "critical stance"—critical reflection regarding society's culture, policy, and practices or critical social analysis; we use the terms critical reflection and critical social analysis interchangeably.

These ideas beg the question of how reflection and action are related. Does critical reflection necessarily lead to action, or are there other ingredients needed to move beyond "armchair activism"? Most scholars and activists would see critical social analysis as necessary for effective political action—people do not participate blindly without some understanding of why they are engaging in political action. What is less clear is whether

NEW DIRECTIONS FOR CHILD AND ADOLESCENT DEVELOPMENT • DOI: 10.1002/cd

critical reflection is *sufficient*. Consider this example from Freire's (1973) book, *Education for Critical Consciousness*, ". . . to every understanding, sooner or later an action corresponds. Once man perceives a challenge, understands it, and *recognizes the possibilities of response* he acts. The nature of that action corresponds to the nature of his understanding" (p. 44, emphasis added).

The phrase "recognizes the possibility of response" suggests that psychological factors influence civic and political behavior. Most scholars and activists would agree that a sense of agency is also necessary for effective political action. That is, people may understand structural inequalities, but not feel compelled to act on their insights unless they believe their efforts will yield a desired outcome. Together, the ideas above suggest a theoretical formulation of critical consciousness that has distinct components—critical social analysis, political efficacy (the perceived ability to effect sociopolitical change), and participation in civic or political action. Because social or political action may influence critical reflection as well as vice versa, there is likely to be a complex relationship between these components.

Freire is revered by progressive scholars, educators, and activists alike because he weaves together critical theory, a philosophy of education, pedagogy, and social change. He is also distinguished by his passion for practice: he was as much a practicing teacher as a theorist. His egalitarian pedagogy values collaboration and rejects sharp hierarchies between teacher and student. He was also critical of "banking" education where the teacher "deposited" knowledge in students, rather than promoting agency and learning through engagement with the world. For him reading, dialogue, reflection, and action were all part of what he called critical consciousness and were key to a new self-understanding in historical, cultural, and political contexts.

Freire's emphasis on consciousness and social justice has roots in ancient wisdom systems such as religion and philosophy. However, European intellectuals such as Marx moved away from notions of karma and the divine and relied instead on emerging social science theory. Marx's theory of dialectic materialism in the late 1800s argued that the consciousness associated with class oppression helps sustain inequality and explains why people engage in actions contrary to their personal and class interests.

Later, the postcolonial era in Africa and the Pacific Islands gave rise to an analysis of colonization—particularly its psychological impact. Albert Memmi and Franz Fanon were among the leading social theorists of this era of the mid-twentieth century. In the United States, Carter Woodson's writings on Black education in the 1930s made a case for how segregation-era schooling served to socialize children into subservient social roles and a sense of inferiority. The major contribution Memmi, Fanon, Woodson, and other early writers made to the CC idea was a cultural and psychological perspective on liberation. In particular, they elaborated how institutional policies and practices contribute to the internalization of oppression. Since the mid-twentieth century, when Freire was developing his ideas, critical social analysis has increasingly relied on a *rights* perspective (human or constitutional). In this view, social injustice is rooted in a deprivation of human or constitutional rights. The United Nations Declaration of Human Rights, the Civil Rights Movement, the Equal Rights Amendment for Women, and the gay rights movement are all examples of the growing rights perspective. As for youth rights, in countries such as South Africa and Northern Ireland, young people have rights to participate in civic and governmental affairs that are protected by national law. This is not the case in the United States, which has not been a world leader in establishing young people's rights. To date, the United States and Somalia remain the only two nations that are not signatories to the United Nations Convention of the Rights of the Child.

The Research Literature on Critical Consciousness

Much of this section will focus on "sociopolitical" theory, constructs, and research that is consistent with critical consciousness writings (e.g., Diemer, Kauffman, Koenig, Trahan, & Hsieh, 2006; Watts & Flanagan, 2007). It provides detail on the three CC components we described early on. Proponents of a sociopolitical perspective on youth civic development, which includes the authors of this chapter, do not always describe their work as critical consciousness theory; nor do proponents of "empowerment" theory, whose ideas we will also describe in this section. According to leading empowerment theorists, empowerment includes ". . . a combination of self-acceptance and self-confidence, social and political understanding, and the ability to play an assertive role in controlling resources and decisions in one's community" (Zimmerman & Rappaport, 1988, p. 726). This is obviously similar to critical social analysis, yet leading authors who write about empowerment do not necessarily mention CC or Freire.

Components of Critical Consciousness. In our view, CC is composed of three components—critical reflection, political efficacy, and critical action. Knowledge of CC and its component parts helps youth practitioners and scholars facilitate the process and expand understanding of the concept. *Critical reflection* refers to a social analysis and moral rejection of societal inequities, such as social, economic, racial/ethnic, and gender inequities that constrain well-being and human agency. Those who are critically reflective view social problems and inequalities in systemic terms. *Political efficacy* is the perceived capacity to effect social and political change by individual and/or collective activism. It follows that people will be much more likely to engage in critical action if they feel that they can create change. *Critical action* refers to individual or collective action taken to change aspects of society, such as institutional policies and practices, which are perceived to be unjust. This is a broad view of activism that includes participation in activities such as voting, community organizing, and peaceful protests.

Freire viewed the relation between reflection and action as reciprocal. Critical reflection is generally considered a precursor to critical action—people do not act to change their social conditions without some consciousness or awareness that their social conditions are unjust. He theorized that as oppressed people begin to analyze their social conditions, they would feel able and compelled to act to change them. Reciprocally, as people act on their social conditions they would gain a more sophisticated understanding of structural oppression. Thus, as critical reflection grows, critical action follows and vice versa in the cyclical process of CC development. However, there will also be times when critical action fails to yield the desired result, which can lead to frustration and cynicism, rather than a greater awareness of societal inequities.

Increasingly, research supports the idea that CC includes critical reflection, critical action, and political efficacy components, and that these components can be measured with marginalized youth of color (e.g., Diemer & Blustein, 2006; Diemer & Li, in press). But what leads critically reflective young people to *act* on their critical reflection sooner rather than later? Research to date does not provide an answer; in our writings we have proposed a sociopolitical theory that lends itself to quantitative approaches. However, instrumentation is in an early phase. Below, we review the conceptualization and measurement of critical reflection, critical action, and political efficacy. We note how these constructs have been measured to help explain them and to guide researchers interested in studying CC with young people and how youth practitioners can think about targeting different components of CC in advocacy training, interventions, and other settings.

Critical Reflection. Of the three components, critical reflection is the most neglected in youth civic engagement research, while being a central component of CC. Therefore, it will receive the most attention here. Rather than limiting analysis to "blaming the victim" and other individualistic explanations for societal inequities, critical reflection results from an analysis of the structural causes of racial/ethnic, socioeconomic, and gendered disparities in health, well-being, educational attainment, wealth, and other domains. It also frames social inequalities in a historical context, with an emphasis on its root *causes*—social structures' policies and practices. Returning to Freire's perspective, "The more accurately men grasp true causality, the more critical their understanding of reality will be" (1973, p. 44).

We found no scales designed especially to measure critical reflection. However, social psychological theories of attribution are particularly relevant to critical reflection research. People make causal attributions to make sense of social problems and inequalities, such as disparities between poor people and rich people. These attributions may be more individual (e.g., we have an equal social system and opportunities, therefore the limited effort and/or ability of groups on the lower rungs of society cause social problems and inequalities) or may be more structural (e.g., we have an unequal social system and opportunities, therefore social systems, policies, and historical conditions cause social problems and inequalities). People with greater levels of critical reflection make more structural attributions for social problems and group disparities.

Neville, Coleman, Falconer, and Holmes (2005) repurposed an existing measure to assess individual and structural attributions for the collective economic and social position of African Americans. Individual attributions were represented by items such as "lack of motivation and unwillingness to work hard" and structural attributions by endorsement of "lack of educational opportunities" and similar items. Neville et al. (2005) observed that individualistic attributions were associated with a "color blind" racial ideology, where the existence of racism is denied or minimized among African American adults. Although these authors did not explicitly align their "attribution of blame" scale with CC theory, or sample young people, we see it a promising approach to assess critical reflection.

Another construct associated with critical social analysis is social dominance orientation (SDO), which refers to the attributions people make for groups' collective social position (Pratto, Sidanius, Stallworth, & Malle, 1994). The SDO scale measures support for group-based inequalities and dominance and has been associated with ideologies such as the "meritocracy myth," racist attitudes, and social Darwinism. If scored in reverse, SDO becomes a measure for the rejection of such views. Sample items include "It's probably a good thing that certain groups are at the top and other groups are at the bottom." Rejection of ideologies that favor social inequality has been associated with greater levels of critical reflection among urban adolescents (Diemer et al., 2006). Similarly, critical reflection (also measured by lower SDO scores) was associated with greater progress in career development among urban adolescents, suggesting that critical reflection may help marginalized youth overcome external barriers to success in school and work (Diemer & Blustein, 2006).

Qualitative and participatory action research has approached the assessment of critical reflection through the identification of themes. Interventions are often part of the endeavor and researchers are more likely to be explicit in their use of CC concepts and terms. As their participants reflect on their lives in their own words, they do not necessarily distinguish these three CC components. Carlson, Engbretson, and Chamberlain (2006) employed a photovoice methodology with both youth and adults of a low-income urban area in the United States, using the participants' explanations of their community photographs as data to explore critical reflection. Their analysis led to a four-stage understanding of critical reflection: (1) passive adaptation, (2) emotional engagement, (3) cognitive awakening, and (4) intention to act. An example of "cognitive awakening" is the increased awareness of connections between local economic activity and community conditions. One participant demonstrated cognitive awakening in her understanding of how poor community conditions are perpetuated by local businesses: "The owners won't participate in, or contribute to, anything we do in the neighborhood. Why do we support them when they grab their children, their fine expensive cars, and our money and dash out of the community before dark every day?" (p. 845). Making this type of attribution for social problems is indicative of more advanced critical reflection.

Action researchers have sought to enhance CC as they learn about it, fostering sociopolitical development among youth in an effort to lessen the risk of negative health or psychosocial outcomes. In a participatory action research project, Stewart, Riecken, Scott, Tanaka, and Riecken (2008)—engaged indigenous Canadian youth in the creation of health information videos. According to the authors, the young people expanded their notions of health literacy to their own cultural traditions, developed a more critical perspective on issues in their community, and some reported changes in their personal health behavior. Watts, Griffith, and Abdul-Adil (1999) coached high school students to decode social messages in "gangsta" rap music videos. All too often, these representations of youth emphasize shortcomings in the character of individuals rather than social systems. Similarly, Campbell and MacPhail's (2002) CC intervention engaged South African youth in discussions of gender roles to help them move the "causal" explanation for human immunodeficiency virus (HIV) infection from a more personal decision-making problem to one that took into consideration cultural norms that pressured young women into unsafe sex. Their work also shows the power of a Freirean approach in helping young people examine their social privilege (e.g, as males, heterosexuals, affluent, etc.) as well as their marginalization. Campbell and MacPhail (2002) recommend that peer HIV education include CC education and reflection, particularly on notions of masculinity and femininity.

The connection between critical reflection on social identity and internalized oppression or privilege is also important. Guessous (2004) and Watts (2010) analyzed young people's applications to a selective, nationally recognized training program for community organizers of color. They found that participants' interest in social justice organizing stemmed from critical values instilled through family in childhood and adolescence, a salient and positive social identity, personal experience with injustice, and critical reflection. Watts' analysis of this dataset suggested a synergy between critical reflection and the rich and varied experiences with social identity and activism in these settings; his findings suggest that researchers need to assess opportunities for civic and political engagement in the social and institutional environment as well as psychological factors in political development.

Political Efficacy. Political efficacy has been studied in political science since the 1950s, generally referring to people's beliefs about their capacity to be effective political actors ("internal political efficacy") and beliefs that government structures and officials are responsive to one's political interests ("external political efficacy") (Morrell, 2003). In this chapter, we use the term political efficacy to connote the perceived capacity to effect social and political change via individual and/or collective activism. Kieffer (1984) similarly argued that "participatory competence," the perceived capacity to effect change, was an important precursor to activism behavior. It follows that people will be much more likely to engage in critical action if they perceive the ability to create change via their actions.

The Sociopolitical Control Scale (SPCS) measures youths' perceived ability to effect social change via political participation and social action (Zimmerman & Zahniser, 1991). A sample (reverse-coded) SPCS item reads, "So many other people are active in local issues and organizations that it doesn't matter much to me whether I participate or not." Generally, the SPCS has demonstrated satisfactory reliability but not always with urban adolescent samples. Nonetheless, it holds promise as a measure of political efficacy. The SPCS is rooted in Kieffer's notion of participatory competence and has been used with youth populations.

Critical Action. Critical action, the third component of critical consciousness, refers to individual or collective action taken to change aspects of society, such as institutional policies and practices, which are perceived to be unjust. We take a broad view of critical action here, encompassing social justice activism (which usually occurs outside of traditional political processes) as well as action taken within the political system to change unjust social conditions and policies. Both forms of action presuppose some degree of critical reflection—that participants view social problems in systemic terms. Critical action is generally measured in quantitative research by the frequency of participation or intentions to participate in social action. Research has devoted less attention to the subjective meaning people attribute to their social and political action, perhaps an avenue for future research.

The Youth Inventory of Involvement (YII) broadly measures youths' participation in political activities and also sports, the arts, and school events (Pancer, Pratt, Hunsberger, & Alisat, 2007). The Political Activities subscale of the YII consists of seven items that measure the frequency of participation in "a protest march, meeting or demonstration" and "preparing and making verbal and written presentations to organizations, agencies, conferences, or politicians." These items measure critical action via participation in more traditional forms of political behavior as well as collective social action. The Political Activities subscale has shown good reliability with a diverse sample of Canadian youth.

NEW DIRECTIONS FOR CHILD AND ADOLESCENT DEVELOPMENT • DOI: 10.1002/cd

The Activism Orientation Scale (AOS) measures how likely people will engage in political action taken to reduce perceived inequities (Corning & Myers, 2002). The conceptual framework of the AOS also takes a broad definition of activist behavior, measuring participation with Conventional Activism and High-Risk Activism subscales. A sample Conventional Activism item asks, "How likely is it that you will attend a political group's organizational meeting?" and a sample High-Risk Activism item asks "How likely is it that you will engage in a political activity in which you suspect there would be a confrontation with the police or possible arrest?" This scale has been shown to be reliable with predominantly White samples of college students, but its usefulness with younger or marginalized populations is unknown.

Comparing Critical Consciousness and Empowerment Theory. As noted earlier, empowerment theory is related to critical consciousness and also overlaps with sociopolitical theory. Typically, empowerment theory examines the experience of collective or personal power that is associated with social change activity. It is also concerned with how community resources such as organizations can foster social power. Psychological empowerment is seen as having cognitive, emotional, and behavioral dimensions, which researchers use to assess an individual's capacity to engage in change activities and the extent to which they actually do so. The Cognitive Empowerment Scale (Peterson, Hamme, & Speer, 2002) assesses the intellectual dimension of psychological empowerment, and it resembles critical reflection but with a greater emphasis on social power. Their "behavioral empowerment" scale parallels the cognitive version by measuring action intended to change community conditions. It is a measure of critical action that asks about behavior such as signing petitions, attending a public meeting to press for policy change, and so on. Research on cognitive and behavioral empowerment indicates that a more sophisticated understanding of community and political power does not predict activism behavior among adults—more evidence that social analysis does not necessarily lead to action, and more findings suggesting that political efficacy may mediate or moderate the relationship between the two.

Differences between the theories are mostly matters of emphasis—both theories include critical reflection, agency, and critical action. Empowerment theory puts less emphasis on an awareness of the structural causes of social problems and social inequality (critical reflection) than does sociopolitical theory. However, the reverse is true with respect to notions of power and agency, which is where empowerment puts its emphasis.

Conclusion

This chapter began by placing critical consciousness in a historical context, to reveal points of departure for contemporary research and practice.

In the second section on research, we noted that many investigators did not view their work as direct extensions of CC theory. Instead, their focus was often describing and understanding psychological concepts associated with the recognition of social injustice and the precursors of action to address it. Yet, researchers have made a number of important contributions to the advancement of CC that we will highlight in this conclusion. The first section looks at the future directions for CC research and theory. The second explores examples and implications for CC practice and action. In both cases, we offer an assessment of progress made to date and our own perspectives on sociopolitical theory.

Future Directions for Critical Consciousness Research and Theory. As Freire's words show, the vocabulary of CC includes history; culture; liberation; oppression (external and internal); social identity; and an integrated perspective on reflection, agency, and political action. As a new area for U.S. social science, CC has not yet matured into well-articulated theory or a coherent body of empirical research. Nonetheless, it has moved in some promising directions. Our review emphasized three core constructs: critical reflection (or critical social analysis), political efficacy (or sense of agency), and critical action. Other ideas in the CC "vocabulary" such as internalized oppression and social identity find expression in the qualitative studies where the voices of young people can be heard and interrelated themes are the units of analysis.

Critical Reflection. In the preceding section, we reviewed promising theoretical and empirical developments in conceptualizing and measuring reflection. What has been given less emphasis, when compared to writings on CC by activist intellectuals, is the role of history. Virtually all organizations engaged in youth organizing see knowledge of history as an essential part of CC.[1] Its temporal dimension helps reveal cause-and-effect relationships between ongoing social forces and current social circumstances. At the moment, we are without a method to assess historical understanding as part of critical social analysis, but qualitative content analysis of interview data offers one way to assess this. Another would be a "quiz" that measures knowledge of significant events (the Stonewall rebellion), movements (women's suffrage), and leaders (Mahatma Gandhi) in social action movements. Recognizing the difficulty in measuring a broad, nuanced historical perspective, quiz scores could serve as a proxy measure of historical perspective.

A different approach to assessing causal reasoning in critical analysis is found in attribution theory and the measurement of attitudes toward social dominance ideology. Attribution theory looks at how what we see as the causes of social problems influences political thinking. Social dominance theory looks at attitudes toward oppressive ideologies. Measures exist for both, and both can be useful in supporting the proposition that young people who attribute social problems to structural injustice and oppressive ideologies (as distinct from endorsing individualistic attributions and a tolerance of social domination) are more likely to engage in social-change activity.

Social Identity. Both sociopolitical and empowerment theory lack a systematic incorporation of social identity. However, there are theories and measures of ethnic; racial; gay, lesbian, bisexual, and transgender (GLBT); and other forms of social identity that could make contributions to CC theory and research. Even a cursory look at social movements and political action shows how social group membership and identity can be a basis for solidarity and collective action. Early research described links between group consciousness and political participation for Blacks, women, and the poor and in later studies between ethnic identity and civic engagement for U.S. immigrant adults (Stepick & Stepick, 2002). Recent research has found that racial group identity and experiences of racial discrimination shape civic behavior (Flanagan, Syvertsen, Gill, Gallay, & Cumsille, 2009). Theory already exists to make the link between social identity and political development. Black racial identity theory includes measures of how members of oppressed social groups (Black people in this case) liberate themselves from oppressive social identities and form new, positive ones. One item on the Nationalist subscale of the Black Racial Identity Scale suggests a direct connection between social identity and critical social analysis: "I believe that the world should be interpreted from a Black perspective" (Sellers, Chavous, & Cooke, 1998). Others (Ginwright & James, 2002) argue that a critical social analysis of internalized and external oppression heals the wounds of social oppression and marginalization.

Empowerment Theory. Although our focus was primarily on sociopolitical theory (i.e., critical reflection, political efficacy, and critical action) as a basis for empirical CC research, we also noted the importance of empowerment theory. Sociopolitical theory is strong on understanding CC's interplay of psychological and behavioral dynamics, while empowerment theory emphasizes an understanding of social power, sense of control, and the settings that foster these factors. Leading empowerment theorists and researchers such as Zimmerman (2000) consider three levels of analysis: individual, organizational, and community. Some versions of sociopolitical theory include the "opportunity structures" young people have for engaging in civic activity, but overall there is less emphasis on settings. In any case, the two theories are not incompatible. For example, the sociopolitical control measure discussed above originated in the empowerment literature. The two theories are complementary in that theorizing about persons and environments is essential to understanding youth engagement.

Implications for Practice and Action. This chapter focused mostly on translating CC ideas to social science theory and empirical study. However, Freire's ideas integrated theory and practice, because he was committed to education for *liberation*. Similarly, Martín-Baró (1994) saw reflection, theory, and action as reciprocal processes rather than categories. It is not coincidental that Freire and Martín-Baró worked in South and Central America rather than the United States. The history of deadly state and paramilitary terror led many to reject experimental social psychology in favor of liberation social psychology and to embrace participatory action research (PAR). We highlighted a few U.S. PAR studies because more is available on work with youth populations, but the bulk of work directly relevant to the practice of CC originates outside of North America. *Psychology of Liberation: Theory and Applications* edited by Montero and Sonn (2009) serves as the single best example. These opening comments on practice are important because the cultural and historical forces influencing the U.S. social sciences are a challenge to an integration of research and practice consistent with CC's social justice origins. Traditionally, the physical sciences (which until recently, the social sciences have emulated) place a premium on objectivity, see researcher effects as a source of error, and privilege the production of new knowledge over the application of existing knowledge. Participatory action researchers have a stance that is contrary to many of these principles, so its proponents in the United States can find themselves on the academic margins. In PAR, knowledge production shares the spotlight with relationships and intervention and the researcher is an active player rather than a source of error variance. Yes, postpositivist traditions have been challenged by critical theory, deconstructionist and postmodern ideas, but activism in the academy is not yet in the mainstream. With these considerations in mind, we look to our colleagues to the south such as Montero, who has extensive experience as professor, activist, and CC practitioner.

It is generally agreed that, in practice, developing critical reflection is a social and process-intensive activity. As Montero (2009) notes, "The conscientization process begins with the people's participation and the discussion–reflection which is part of the sequence action–reflection–action (in organized community groups or in other forms of gathering). This supposes a variety of ways to problematize naturalized modes of understanding and interpreting daily life and events happening within it. Problematization is a way to challenge accepted explanations for those phenomena that have been assumed as normal and logical in daily life, but which make people's lives difficult; even painful, unfair, and hard" (p. 78).

If there is a single term that captures CC practice, it is *group discussion*. To be successful according to Montero, there must be listening, dialog, humility, respect, and critique. The aim is to come close to consensus on the problematization of recurring aspects of everyday experience. From there, young people begin to consider solutions aimed at the sociopolitical roots of the problem. It should be evident how this activity brings together attribution theory, a historical-cultural perspective, and the affairs of everyday life shared by the group participants. Sociopolitical and empowerment theory would contend that political efficacy or a psychological sense of power must be cultivated along with this process to move young people toward critical action on the problem.

In the spirit of Freire's work, U.S. researchers should consider collaborative methods and a social justice stance in their study of youth civic and political engagement. Tracing the development of CC and related topics over time (e.g., internalized oppression, historical analysis, and social identity) benefits from authentic, egalitarian, and mutually beneficial relationships. Case study and mixed-method longitudinal research can identify and help cross-validate core CC constructs, while narrative and participant observation methods complement knowledge gained from quantitative studies. All of this requires time and commitment by the host organization. Because social justice is a core value in youth organizations engaged in social-change work, they tend to be especially responsive to the collaborative features of participatory research methods. Watts offers one concrete example of this from his experience with PAR. In a PAR project he supervised, young people were upset about the taste and nutrition of cafeteria food in their schools. As the group discussion progressed, it became evident that students attending schools in higher-income areas had well-stocked salad bars, while those in marginalized areas had none. Two things happened as time went on: young people came to see their everyday experience of low-quality food as problematic rather than "just the way it is," but as a group they also came to see between-school inequalities in food quality as problematic. Critical social analysis of this inequality included their racial and social class identities. Graduate students worked with these high school students to conduct a study of the problem among peers and stakeholders and helped them create a presentation for school administrators aimed at change in food-service policies.

Youth sociopolitical interventions and the facilitation of critical reflection groups are within the scope of many human service and university-based personnel, but community organizers are the specialists in critical action (see endnote for leading examples). However, only recently have organizers made a systematic effort to include youth development outcomes as well as political outcomes to their mission. Political work can be stressful, and there is a hazard in boosting critical social analysis in young people without raising political efficacy at the same time. An expanded awareness of entrenched social problems without a sense of agency or the organizing skills to set and achieve attainable objectives can lead young people to feel overwhelmed and demoralized. Thus, a holistic approach to working with young people and teamwork across areas of specialty is essential. Young people are a precious social resource in a stage of rapid development. Researchers and practitioners in the social sciences can contribute to youth civic development by filling the gap between youth socio-emotional development and political competence.

References

Campbell, C., & MacPhail, C. (2002). Peer education, gender and the development of critical consciousness: Participatory HIV prevention by South African youth. *Social Science and Medicine, 55*(2), 331–345. doi:10.1016/S0277-9536(01)00289-1

Carlson, E. D., Engbretson, J., & Chamberlain, R. M. (2006). Photovoice as a social process of critical consciousness. *Qualitative Health Research, 16*(6), 836–852. doi:10.1177/1049732306287525

Corning, A. F., & Myers, D. J. (2002). Individual orientation toward engagement in social action. *Political Psychology, 23*(4), 703–729. doi:10.1111/0162-895X.00304

Diemer, M. A., & Blustein, D. L. (2006). Critical consciousness and career development among urban youth. *Journal of Vocational Behavior, 68*(2), 220–232. doi:10.1016/j.jvb.2005.07.001

Diemer, M. A., Kauffman, A., Koenig, N., Trahan, E., & Hsieh, C. (2006). Challenging racism, sexism, and social injustice: Support for urban adolescents' critical consciousness development. *Cultural Diversity and Ethnic Minority Psychology, 12*(3), 444–460.

Diemer, M. A. & Li, C. (in press). Critical consciousness and political engagement among marginalized youth. *Child Development.*

Flanagan, C. A., Syvertsen, A. K., Gill, S., Gallay, L. S., & Cumsille, P. (2009). Ethnic awareness, prejudice, and civic commitments in four ethnic groups of American adolescents. *Journal of Youth and Adolescence, 38*(4), 500–518. doi:10.1007/s10964-009-9394-z

Freire, P. (1973). *Education for critical consciousness.* New York, NY: Seabury.

Ginwright, S., & James, T. (2002). From assets to agents of change: Social justice, organizing, and youth development. In B. Kirshner, J. L. O'Donoghue, & M. McLaughlin (Eds.), Youth participation: Improving institutions and communities. *New Directions for Youth Development, 2002*(96), 27–46. doi:10.1002/yd.25

Guessous, O. (2004). *The sociopolitical development of community and labor organizers of color: A qualitative study* (Unpublished master's thesis). Georgia State University, Atlanta.

Kieffer, C. H. (1984). Citizen empowerment: A developmental perspective. *Prevention in Human Services, 3,* 9–36.

Martín-Baró, I. (1994). *Writings for a Liberation Psychology.* Cambridge, MA: Harvard University Press.

Montero, M. (2009). Methods for liberation: Critical consciousness in action. In M. Montero & C. Sonn (Eds.), *Psychology of liberation: Theory and applications* (pp. 73–92). New York, NY: Springer.

Montero, M., & Sonn, C. (Eds.). (2009). *Psychology of liberation: Theory and applications.* New York, NY: Springer.

Morrell, M. E. (2003). Survey and experimental evidence for a reliable and valid measure of internal political efficacy. *Public Opinion Quarterly, 67,* 589–602.

Neville, H. A., Coleman, M. N., Falconer, J. W., & Holmes, D. (2005). Color-blind racial ideology and psychological false consciousness among African Americans. *Journal of Black Psychology, 31*(1), 27–45. doi:10.1177/0095798404268287

Pancer, S. M., Pratt, M., Hunsberger, B., & Alisat, S. (2007). Community and political involvement in adolescence: What distinguishes the activists from the uninvolved? *Journal of Community Psychology, 35,* 741–759. doi:10.1002/jcop.20176

Peterson, N. A., Hamme, C. L., & Speer, P. W. (2002). Cognitive empowerment of African Americans and Caucasians: Differences in understandings of power, political functioning, and shaping ideology. *Journal of Black Studies, 32*(3), 332–347. doi:10.1177/002193470203200304

Pratto, F., Sidanius, J., Stallworth, L. M., & Malle, B. F. (1994). Social dominance orientation: A personality variable predicting social and political attitudes. *Journal of Personality and Social Psychology, 67*(4), 741–763.

Sellers, R. M., Chavous, T. M., & Cooke, D. Y. (1998). Racial ideology and racial centrality as predictors of African American college students' academic performance. *Journal of Black Psychology, 24*(1), 8–27. doi:10.1177/00957984980241002

Stepick, A., & Stepick, C. (2002). Becoming American, constructing ethnicity: Immigrant youth and civic engagement. *Applied Developmental Science, 6*(4), 246–257. doi: 10.1207/S1532480XADS0604_12

Stewart, S., Riecken, T., Scott, T., Tanaka, M., & Riecken, J. (2008). Expanding health literacy: Indigenous youth creating videos. *Journal of Health Psychology, 13,* 180–189. doi: 10.1177/1359105307086709

Watts, R. (2010). *Learning principles for political and civic education from young activists.* Chicago, IL: The Spencer Foundation.

Watts, R. J., & Flanagan, C. (2007). Pushing the envelope on youth civic engagement: A developmental and liberation psychology perspective. *Journal of Community Psychology, 35*(6), 779–792. doi:10.1002/jcop.20178

Watts, R. J., Griffith, D. M., & Abdul-Adil, J. (1999). Sociopolitical development as an antidote for oppression—theory and action. *American Journal of Community Psychology, 27*(2), 255–271. doi:10.1023/A:1022839818873

Westheimer, J., & Kahne, J. (2003). Teaching democracy: What schools need to do. *Phi Delta Kappan, 85*(1), 34–40, 57–66.

Zimmerman, M. (2000). Empowerment theory: Psychological, organizational, and community levels of analysis. In J. Rappaport & E. Seidman (Eds.), *Handbook of community psychology* (pp. 43–63). New York, NY: Kluwer.

Zimmerman, M., & Rappaport, J. (1988). Citizen participation, perceived control, and psychological empowerment. *American Journal of Community Psychology, 16,* 725–750. doi:10.1007/BF00930023

Zimmerman, M. A., & Zahniser, J. H. (1991). Refinements of sphere-specific measures of perceived control: Development of a sociopolitical control scale. *Journal of Community Psychology, 19,* 189–204. doi:10.1002/1520-6629(199104)19:2<189::AID-JCOP2290190210>3.0.CO;2-6

Note

1. Stand-out examples include the School of Unity and Liberation (SOUL), Education for Liberation, PICO National Network, the Movement Strategy Center, the Brotherhood/Sister Sol, and Project South.

RODERICK J. WATTS *is professor of social work and psychology at Hunter College and the Graduate Center at City University of New York. E-mail: rwatts@gc.cuny.edu*

MATTHEW A. DIEMER *is associate professor of counseling, educational psychology, and special education at Michigan State University, East Lansing. E-mail: diemerm@msu.edu*

ADAM M. VOIGHT *is a PhD student in human and organizational development at Vanderbilt University in Nashville, Tennessee. E-mail: adam.voight@vanderbilt.edu*

Seif, H. (2011). "Unapologetic and unafraid": Immigrant youth come out from the shadows. In C. A. Flanagan & B. D. Christens (Eds.), Youth civic development: Work at the cutting edge. New Directions for Child and Adolescent Development, 134, 59–75.

5

"Unapologetic and Unafraid": Immigrant Youth Come Out From the Shadows

Hinda Seif

Abstract

Young immigrants are challenging the boundaries of citizenship and insisting on their human rights. This chapter examines the civic lives of immigrant youth through the case of Latina/os, exploring the paradox of their apparent low civic education and engagement levels and remarkable participation in recent protests. After an overview of demographics and what we know about immigrant youth civic life, the focus shifts to the undocumented. Many retain a sense of community obligation, yet because of their developmental stage and U.S. education, their engagement differs from that of their parents' generation. Young immigrants are reconfiguring organizing and reenergizing U.S. democracy through their use of new information technologies. © 2011 Wiley Periodicals, Inc.

This research was conducted with the support of the Center for State Policy and Leadership, University of Illinois at Springfield. Special thanks to the staff and members of the Illinois Coalition for Immigrant and Refugee Rights (ICIRR), who labored for the passage of the Illinois DREAM Act.

In spring 2006, three and a half to five million people marched throughout the United States against a congressional proposal to criminalize undocumented immigrants and for comprehensive immigration reform (Bada, Fox, & Selee, 2006). More than half of the recent immigration reform protesters may be under 28 (Bloemraad & Trost, 2008; Flores-Gonzáles, 2010). High school students quickly spread the word about school walkouts by text-messaging, sometimes covertly in class. Participants carried signs and wore T-shirts that proclaimed, "We Are All Immigrants," blurring boundaries between immigrants and U.S.-born youth. In December 2010, President Obama proclaimed that a great disappointment of the last congressional session was the failure to pass the DREAM (Development, Relief, and Education for Alien Minors) Act, a bill to provide a pathway to legalization for undocumented youth who were raised in the United States. Although the bill failed in the Senate, for the first time since DREAM Act legislation was originally introduced in 2001, it passed the House of Representatives that year. This partial legislative victory followed an unprecedented campaign led by affected youth and their allies of letter writing, petitioning, and organizing rallies; hunger strikes; and acts of civil disobedience. More and more young people born abroad are publicly "coming out" with the battle cry "undocumented, unapologetic, and unafraid"!

Immigrant youth are at the cutting edge of civic engagement in the United States today. Attacks against immigrants and racial profiling are increasingly impacting all young Latina/os, but they are especially difficult for the foreign-born. Some immigrant youth are less likely to take for granted U.S. civic and economic opportunities compared to their U.S.-born peers. As one of the first demographics to take advantage of new information technologies such as texting, Facebook, YouTube, and Twitter to mobilize a political movement, young immigrants are also reconfiguring the speed, scope, and form of organizing (Yang, 2007). Yet because they face great barriers to civic development and participation, on average, Latina/o immigrant youth are less likely to become engaged than their citizen peers.

In this chapter, I examine what we know about the civic lives of immigrant youth through the case of Latina/os, the largest foreign-born population in the United States. I explore the paradox of their apparent low general civic education and engagement levels and extraordinary participation in recent protests. First, the demographics of Latina/o youth immigration are examined and why the civic development of Latina/o youth is so crucial for a healthy U.S. democracy. After an overview of what we know about immigrant youth civic life, the focus shifts to the case of undocumented youth. Young immigrants are challenging the boundaries of citizenship and insisting on their human rights by becoming civic actors, even when they are not citizens or even in the United States legally. Although their civic participation overlaps with that of older immigrants

NEW DIRECTIONS FOR CHILD AND ADOLESCENT DEVELOPMENT • DOI: 10.1002/cd

and citizen youth, it is also distinctive. Because of their developmental stage and their experience of being educated and instructed about U.S. civics, their engagement differs from that of their parents' generation in form and substance.

Demographic Patterns of Latina/o Youth

Young Latina/o immigrants and their civic activity are in the spotlight for demographic and political reasons. The expansion of free trade agreements, the implementation of neoliberal policies, civil and drug wars south of the border, and the disruption of cross-border circular migration patterns have fueled an increase in Latina/o immigration. Latina/os are currently the largest minority group in the United States, and the health of democracy in this country will increasingly depend on the quality of their civic participation. Although the proportion of "non-Hispanic White" youth decreases, 23 percent of all persons under 18 are now Latina/o (Passel, Cohn, & Hugo Lopez, 2011). As Latina/o immigrants disperse from traditional immigrant-receiving regions, they are increasingly visible throughout the country.

In 2009, foreign-born youth constituted 6 percent of minors between the ages of twelve and seventeen (Passel, 2011). Most immigrant youth hail from Latin America and the Hispanic Caribbean. In 2006, 64 percent of those born abroad between the ages of sixteen and twenty-five were Latina/o, with 42 percent from Mexico, 16 percent from Central America, and 6 percent from South America (Marcelo & Lopez, 2006). Immigrant youth demographic and settlement patterns do not mirror those of older immigrants. For example, they are more likely to live in suburbs and in the South (Marcelo & Lopez, 2006). We cannot generalize about immigrant youth civic life through the case of Latina/os, who are the most likely to have parents with little formal education, live in poverty, and lack legal U.S. status. Youth of Asian ancestry appear to be more likely to be civically engaged than White and Black American youth (Marcelo, Lopez, & Kirby, 2007).

Because of increasingly stringent immigration laws and the failure to enact a large-scale legalization of the undocumented since 1986, compared to older immigrants, young immigrants are more likely to be noncitizens and lack lawful U.S. status. Since 1986, the last large-scale legalization, it has become increasingly difficult for young immigrants to legalize their status. In 2009, almost half of U.S. youth between the ages of twelve and seventeen who were born abroad, or 2.4 percent of all U.S. youth in that age range, were also undocumented. More than half of Latina/o immigrant children lack U.S. legal status, and this proportion rises for older youth (Passel, 2011). Undocumented youth cannot be lawfully excluded from public kindergarten through grade twelve (K–12) education. Thus, in late adolescence many Latina/o immigrants are grappling with coming of age as "illegal aliens" after being raised and educated, including receiving civic training, alongside citizen peers. Their social exclusion intensifies with age, and increasingly impacts their fellow students, teachers and school staff, and classroom dynamics as they progress from one grade to the next. Their civic lives are shaped by the contradiction between their high motivation to forge a new life and better opportunities for family and community in the United States and their restricted membership in a society where they are classified as "illegal."

Immigrant Youth Diversity. Interest in immigrant youth civic life has blossomed since 2000, spurred by in-state tuition and DREAM Act organizing. Yet civic patterns vary because of the great diversity of young immigrants. Some are recent arrivals (first generation) and others were born abroad yet primarily educated in U.S. schools (called the "1.5 generation"). The experiences of immigrant youth also diverge depending on whether they are U.S. citizens, lawful permanent residents, undocumented, or have pending immigration applications or other forms of intermediate status.

Latina/o immigrant youth are diverse in many other ways. Some consider English their primary language and others are English-language learners. Young immigrants come from many countries and language groups: they may be Zapotec speakers from a highland village in Oaxaca or mestizo *chilangos* from Mexico City. They live in rural towns in the U.S. South or West, in Midwest meatpacking communities, in Northeast urban centers, and in mid-Atlantic suburbs. Youth live in racially segregated communities, in "ghettos" transforming from Black to Latino majorities, and in affluent White suburbs. Many undocumented youth never visit their countries of origin, and other young immigrants summer with family abroad. Some retain links to indigenous languages and cultures; others do not.

Since Proposition 187, a California voter initiative that would have required proof of lawful U.S. status to enroll in public K–12 schools, immigration politics have been blurring the border between immigrant and nonimmigrant youth identities in a phenomenon called "reactive ethnicity" (Portes & Bach, 1985). Waves of xenophobia have led more second-generation students to identify themselves as "immigrants" and challenge the boundaries that separate them from immigrants in their families, schools, and neighborhoods (Flores-Gonzáles, 2010). Although this chapter focuses on foreign-born youth, the more Latina/o immigrants are oppressed by prejudice and policy, the more their issues, difficulties, and perspectives appear to be shared by young, U.S.-born Latina/os.

Lower Apparent Civic Engagement, High Ethnic Participation

Immigrant youth civic development and participation takes place in families, schools, communities, and political institutions. Schools have long had a special role in orienting the children of immigrants to U.S. nationalism and civic life. Unlike many public arenas such as the workplace, voting booth, and highways, where the undocumented face legal sanctions, youth have access to K-12 public schools regardless of their immigration status. The U.S. Supreme Court's *Plyler v. Doe* decision (1982), which protected this access, focused on the potential role of undocumented youth in civic life. In the court's majority opinion, Justice William Brennan declared that "[b]y denying these children a basic education, we deny them the ability to live within the structure of our civic institutions, and foreclose any realistic possibility that they will contribute in even the smallest way to the progress of our Nation" (pp. 223–224).

Historically, educators, activists, and scholars have debated whether immigrant education in the United States, including learning for civic participation, should aim toward their assimilation into dominant culture and society, or whether a key pathway for their active social engagement is through ethnic identities, affiliations, and knowledge. Scholars including Valenzuela (1999) find that a subtractive paradigm, where young immigrants and the second generation are compelled to forfeit their language and culture of ancestry, has negative consequences for their education; this is also true for their civic engagement. As for the political arena, although minors and noncitizens are unable to vote, the 2006 immigration protests and the DREAM Act mobilizations demonstrate that some immigrant youth find powerful ways to voice their political opinions about their families and co-ethnic communities. Their limited socioeconomic capital and immigration status translates into comparatively low understandings of civic concepts and limited political communication skills (Torney-Purta, Barber, & Wilkenfeld 2006) in a power structure dominated by Anglo interests and racial prejudices. Their participation levels are also lower than average in many traditional civic and political forms such as volunteering, electoral activities, and political voice activities such as contacting an elected official and signing a petition (Lopez & Marcelo, 2008; Stepick, Dutton Stepick, & Labissiere, 2008). However, Latina/o immigrant adolescents display strong ethnic and immigrant identities and are likely to support opportunities and rights for immigrants (Torney-Purta et al., 2006). Latina/o immigrant students, with their co-ethnic peers, participated in waves of school walkouts in 1968 and the late 1980s to early 1990s. Students have protested the lack of cultural competence and underfunding in schools that result in low academic achievement and high dropout rates, as well as policies to dismantle bilingual education and ban undocumented students from public education (Seif, 2004; Valenzuela, 1999). In a survey conducted after the 2006 immigration marches, over 23 percent of young immigrants reported that they had participated in a demonstration over the past 12 months (Lopez & Marcelo, 2008).

Immigrant youth participate in other activities that benefit their ethnic groups. Students serve as a cultural bridge by tutoring, assisting other immigrants, and providing linguistic and cultural translation between older immigrants and the host society (Reynolds & Orellana, 2009; Stepick et al., 2008). Translation responsibilities are a double-edged sword increasingly thrust upon Latina/o youth when public services are cut. Children are sometimes forced to interpret sensitive medical information and racist or condescending communications to their parents. Yet youth may feel empowered through speaking up and assisting others. Because older immigrant children are generally more proficient in the languages of their country of origin than their younger, U.S.-born siblings, translations are often performed by undocumented youth. With the increasing diversity of Latin American immigration, in addition to translating between English and Spanish, some young immigrants interpret indigenous languages such as Zapoteco (Reynolds & Orellana, 2009). Foreign-born youth, especially newcomers, also report high involvement in sports, where English language skills are less essential, as well as in church and family activities (Stepick et al., 2008).

Cultural values also generate civic participation. Providing opportunities for the next generation is a driving force of immigration. When parents make sacrifices, their children's success is defined by their ability to elevate their families and communities. These special motivations for immigrant youth are widely acknowledged in relation to their educational success, but they can also lead to civic and political engagement (Brodkin, 2007; Seif, 2004). Latina/o immigrants come from communally oriented cultures that challenge the individualism and nuclear family orientation of U.S. society. For Mexicans, the principle of *educación* "refers to the family's role of inculcating in children a sense of moral, social, and personal responsibility and serves as the foundation for all other learning. . . ." (Valenzuela, 1999, p. 23). *Educación* is the responsibility of families, in addition to schools, and emphasizes collective goals. This cultural standard contributes to the robust civic engagement of some young Mexican immigrants.

Regarding the diversity of immigrant youth, students' participation in extracurricular and civic activities varies depending on their gender and class, church involvement, and level of Americanization (Valenzuela, 1999). As previously noted, eldest siblings generally provide translation because they retain the most Latin American linguistic and cultural knowledge. Girls are most likely to help others, and participating in extracurricular activities is a way to escape strict parents' constant scrutiny. For newcomers, limited English language ability is a barrier to extracurricular participation. Members of the 1.5-generation who are culturally assimilated yet bilingual and who retain pride in their heritage are the most likely immigrant students to participate in mainstream extracurricular activities (Valenzuela, 1999).

As for ethnic variations among Latina/o immigrant youth, the Salvadoran young adult population has reached a critical mass, and their activism appears to be highly transnational compared to that of young Mexican immigrants. The Salvadoran University Student Union (USEA) is the first organization serving Salvadoran students and plays a key role in politicizing and organizing young Salvadorans in California (Perla, 2010). Founded at the University of El Salvador in 2005, several students born in El Salvador and the United States brought the organization back to their Southern California campuses in 2007 after they travelled to a political conference in San Salvador (Perla, 2010). The student organization quickly expanded; with chapters statewide, it aims to spread to other states. The USEA students organize annual conferences that bring together students, activists, and community members to address key issues facing Salvadoran youth such as the impact of civil war traumas on the young generation, and how to conceptualize a transnational Salvadoran identity, succeed academically, and fight for immigrant rights. California student members are also engaged in the well-being and politics of El Salvador.

In sum, although immigrant youth civic education and engagement varies related to characteristics such as length of time in the United States and country of origin, respecting and valuing their connection to their immigrant and co-ethnic identities, families, and communities supports, rather than detracts, from their civic development. They are especially ripe for participating in efforts that promote opportunities and social justice for these populations.

Undocumented Youth: Graduation as Trauma and Performing Model Citizenship

The assumption that people possess freedom of mobility and action is highly problematic for young undocumented immigrants. They are even more likely than their counterparts with papers to be limited by poverty, social segregation, enrollment in low-performing schools, and lack of English language fluency. They may also be motivated to help other immigrants and co-ethnics and to fight for social justice. Yet their constant vulnerability to deportation makes daily life, let alone civic participation, very difficult. Maturing youth without lawful residence are excluded from certain educational and training programs and may need to work illegally. They are generally ineligible for a driver's license and may be unable to join their friends for nighttime entertainment that requires identification. Their lives in the United States are full of fear—of sharing details of their identities with friends and educators and of drawing attention. Many youth in this situation display high levels of stress and anxiety (Perez, Espinoza, Ramos, Coronado, & Cortés, 2009).

Young immigrants find themselves in the eye of a perfect political storm. During tough economic times, immigration is used as a political wedge issue. Republicans introduce draconian laws that target "illegal" immigrants to mobilize their older, European American base in elections, and Democrats use pro-immigrant policies to motivate Latina/o citizens to vote. Policies that impact immigrant youth and their families are being introduced at the federal, state, and local levels. Yet there is some public sympathy for immigrant youth, who are seen as innocent of their parents' migration decisions. Compared to their parents who generally toil at low-wage jobs and speak little English, young immigrants may speak English, excel at school, and symbolize the American dream of social mobility and active civic participation that is threatened for the middle class today. Recent, successful political efforts to improve the lives of immigrants have generally highlighted youth.

Because undocumented children cannot be barred from K–12 schools, they are full members of school society, unlike their parents who are "illegal" in many public and government realms. Their awareness of their own legal status and that of family members varies; some parents inform their children early and others try to shield them from the trauma of undocumented status until the last possible moment: when it is time to fill out college applications, find a job, or learn to drive. Yet as minors, they have a student identity and are less reliant than older persons on Social Security numbers and driver's licenses. These youth are linked to teachers, peers, counselors, and other citizen networks. They serve their neighborhoods, develop leadership skills, and form robust attachments to the United States and its citizens. For example, undocumented students become volunteers through school clubs (Perez, Espinoza, Ramos, Coronado, & Cortés, 2010), where they tend to serve co-ethnics and immigrants and assist with translation (Rogers, Saunders, Terriquez, & Velez, 2008). Despite feeling socially rejected, pursuing rigorous academic curricula, and working more than average, undocumented college students also report a higher than average rate of civic activity (Perez et al., 2010).

Students without green cards face a contradiction between their educational inclusion and their exclusion from other social arenas. Until they reach high school, many know little of their legal status or the difficulties that await them. Rather than a joyful rite of passage, graduation signifies a traumatic change in status and identity from student to socially stigmatized "illegal alien" and illegal worker. Its approach may drive youth to despair or action.

How do we account for the paradox of high civic action despite extraordinary odds? Rather than give into hopelessness, some students volunteer and become politically active. Their community service reflects their commitment to social and political justice. It is also a way for students to resist marginalization and prove to themselves and others than they are model citizens who deserve to be full Americans (Perez et al., 2010).

Yet undocumented students may feel marginalized in organizations that do not focus on their issues. Many Latina/o student groups overlook immigrant concerns (S.I.N. Collective, 2007), and immigrant groups neglect youth and student needs (Gonzales, 2008). The undocumented

NEW DIRECTIONS FOR CHILD AND ADOLESCENT DEVELOPMENT • DOI: 10.1002/cd

may be afraid to reveal their legal status, or their special issues may be swept aside. Young immigrants have started student clubs, organizations, and subcommittees that focus on their specific issues and advocate for policy changes. Despite the harsh economic and political climate, their efforts have had an impact. Through the movement to enact state legislation that qualifies some undocumented college students to pay the equivalent of in-state tuition, as of 2011, laws have been passed or enacted in thirteen states to enable more undocumented students to attend college. Members of immigrant youth groups helped conduct unprecedented organizing drives for passage of the DREAM Act. Through their political activism, young immigrants have forged alternative identities to the stigmatized label of "illegal alien."

The Higher Education Access and In-State Tuition Movement

Although the undocumented cannot legally be excluded from public K–12 schools, their access to higher education is more uncertain and has become a focal point for immigrant youth activism. Seif (2004) examined the successful struggle for California's in-state tuition bill, Assembly Bill (AB) 540, which, when enacted in 2001, became the second law that enabled students who attend the state's high schools for at least three years and graduate to pay the equivalent of in-state tuition at its public colleges and universities regardless of their immigration status. Undocumented teens have emerged as leaders in immigrant communities because of their high educational achievement compared to their parents, their English language abilities, their accepted identity as students, and the mentoring that some receive from second-generation Latina/o educators and activists. Beyond being personally painful, their illegal status and restricted college access demoralizes teachers and fellow students, and robs communities of their young leaders' full potential. Many Latina/o legislators who have supported immigrant-youth-friendly bills identify with 1.5-generation activists because of their own working class and immigrant roots and histories of youthful political engagement (Seif, 2004).

As the struggle for in-state tuition spreads, immigrant youth play key roles in efforts to pass related bills in states including Texas (Rincón, 2008) and Kansas (Reich & Mendoza, 2008). High-achieving immigrant youth, including valedictorians, have emerged from the shadows and garnered public sympathy by telling their personal stories (Rincón, 2008; Seif, 2004). Many stress their civic contributions in verbal and written accounts. Offering testimony empowers youth who have felt ashamed of their legal status by converting their private plight into a political issue (S.I.N. Collective, 2007). They speak at campus rallies, recount their life histories to journalists, lobby, and testify at government hearings. Young activists become engaged despite the hazards. They must overcome their fears and assess the danger of deportation. To minimize risk, many undocumented youth participate in groups with members of mixed immigration statuses, use pseudonyms, and gauge where they can travel safely. Yet they are committed to speaking for themselves.

College access victories, such as in-state tuition laws and the 2011 passage of the Illinois DREAM Act, a bill that further extends higher education access for undocumented students by setting up a mechanism for the state to raise private scholarship funds for this purpose, suggest that regional, pro-immigrant laws can be enacted when they are associated with the faces and stories of accomplished, civic-minded youth (Rincón, 2008; Seif, 2004). As the economy has worsened and opposition to immigration has become more vocal and organized, it has become harder to pass in-state tuition bills and new laws are threatened. In a 2005 effort to pass a bill in North Carolina, letters were circulated from impacted students describing their achievements and aspirations. Yet the bill quickly died because of early, strong, and menacing disagreement. Conservative talk radio played a key role in swiftly inflaming opponents, and some legislators and organizations that supported the bill received threats (Sanders, 2010).

Immigrant Student Groups

New in-state tuition laws have enabled thousands of young adults to attend college, empowered them, and generated more activism (Rincón, 2008; S.I.N. Collective, 2007; Seif, 2010). Youth are creating new self-understandings, enforcing these laws and working to expand their scope, organizing for federal legalization, and engaging in political efforts to help other marginalized groups. Since the California bill's passage, some undocumented youth call themselves *AB 540 students* (Abrego, 2008) or DREAMers. These identifications highlight their positive social roles as students and their relationship to political struggles. They demonstrate how policy proposals that support immigrant youth can mobilize political constituencies and offer powerful opportunities to forge positive identities that challenge the stigma of growing up as an illegal alien.

When undocumented students attend college, they are more likely to remain active in civic life. Youth who helped bring these in-state tuition bills to victory are inspired to further involvement. College-educated immigrants gain more skills and opportunities for engagement compared to their nonmatriculated counterparts. Because of the contradiction between their academic preparation and ineligibility for legal employment, they are poised for activism (Gonzales, 2008; Seif, 2010). Undocumented college students are largely ineligible for government loans and grants, so they often must build social networks and fundraise to pay their tuition. Students wash cars and sell community dinner and raffle tickets, with proceeds funding their schooling (Pérez Huber, 2010).

College campuses have become sites of dynamic immigrant activism. Campus-based networks have formed across the United States that focus on the needs of undocumented students. These organizations educate about their plight; advocate for relevant policies and laws; and, in states where in-state tuition laws have passed, conduct outreach to inform other immigrant youth of college affordability. Through these groups, students advocate for their rights, hold educational forums, gather petitions, and organize mock graduations (Gonzales, 2008; Madera, 2008; Rincón, 2008; S.I.N. Collective, 2007; Seif, 2010). In California, the in-state tuition law has been poorly implemented by schools and government. The first wave of students who benefited from the legislation formed AB 540 associations to enforce the law; organize younger students; and conduct outreach to raise awareness of the new law with parents, high schools, and community-based organizations. These groups formed the AB 540 College Access Network.

The Students Informing Now (S.I.N.) Collective at the University of California, Santa Cruz provides a safe space where undocumented students can share their identities and where their concerns are central (S.I.N. Collective, 2007). Because their group includes students with varied citizenship statuses, members can speak publicly about the plight of undocumented students without revealing their own situation. The group provides family-style support for students who struggle to stay in college and face an uncertain future. Students help each other emotionally, financially, academically, and with transportation. For example, they fundraise to help students stay in school. Student groups in California and across the nation have engaged with state-level policy by defending existing in-state tuition laws, fending off new restrictive legislative proposals and lawsuits, and working to further expand immigrant higher education access.

Immigrant student groups have emerged as important incubators for undocumented youth as active civic participants. Although student organizations such as Improving Dreams, Equality, Access, and Success (IDEAS) at the University of California, Los Angeles have provided extraordinary service given their very limited resources and power, their efforts are no substitute for institutional enforcement of immigrant students' educational rights.

DREAM Act and DREAMers

Some of the most creative, courageous, and effective organizing in the contemporary United States has been conducted by undocumented youth in support of the federal DREAM Act. Each bill introduced since 2001 has proposed that immigrant youth of "good moral character" who live in the United States for at least five years and graduate from U.S. high schools or the equivalent would become eligible to apply for six-year conditional

New Directions for Child and Adolescent Development • DOI: 10.1002/cd

resident status. Their legal status could become permanent upon completion of two years of college or military service. Approximately 755,000 young immigrants would have eventually achieved permanent resident status if the 2010 DREAM Act had passed (Migration Policy Institute, 2010). Over 80 percent of potential beneficiaries are Latina/o, including 62 percent from Mexico (Batalova & McHugh, 2010).

Immigrant youth have been central to gaining support for the DREAM Act by humanizing the plight of the undocumented. This federal legislative effort has become a focus of immigrant youth organizing and is transforming the nature and scope of immigrant activism. Organizations dedicated to passing the bill and fighting for the human and civil rights of the young undocumented have emerged across the country. These groups are affiliated with high schools and higher education institutions, nonprofit organizations, or are independent. They have formed regional networks such as the California DREAM Network, the New York State Youth Leadership Council, and the Student Immigrant Movement in Massachusetts. National networks include DreamActivist.org and United We DREAM.

The in-state tuition struggle laid an important foundation for DREAM organizing. Students across the country had already been involved in the fight for their college access. This activism, including enforcement efforts in states with in-state tuition laws, created networks of experienced youth organizers. Furthermore, the in-state tuition movement produced skilled immigrant college students with severely restricted future options unless the laws changed to legalize their status. In-state efforts also envisioned undocumented youth as students, productive community members, and activists. This groundwork was potently combined with the widespread use of information technologies and social media in which youth are especially fluent, including Facebook, texting, Twitter, and YouTube. The result has been vital virtual and ground organizing.

Inspired by the election of Barack Obama and a new Congress, DREAM activism escalated in 2008. Youth have organized for the bill using traditional methods such as interviewing with the press, placing pressure through petitions and phone call mobilizations, and meeting with elected officials in their home states. With the support of advocacy organizations and private fundraising, young immigrants have also travelled to Washington, D.C. to lobby, protest, and testify in congressional hearings. DREAM organizing has become increasingly creative, bold, and effective. Although those against its passage inundated legislators with their faxes and letters after the terrorists attacks on September 11, 2001, in 2010, DREAM activists also organized massive public support for their cause. Between September and December, pro-immigrant groups generated over 840,000 phone calls, faxes, and e-mails in favor of the DREAM Act, and more than 81,000 petitions were delivered to targeted senate offices (National Immigration Law Center, 2010).

NEW DIRECTIONS FOR CHILD AND ADOLESCENT DEVELOPMENT • DOI: 10.1002/cd

Radical, Coalitional, and Digital Activism

Youth DREAM Act organizing has taken less conventional forms that address intersectional identities and political commitments, utilize virtual platforms, and include creative and militant actions. Students have performed mock graduations locally and at state and federal capitals. Especially since 2009, undocumented students and their allies have resorted to radical activism. Inspired by the civil rights, Chicano, and farm worker movements, they have staged long distance walks and organized sit-ins and hunger strikes, sometimes in front of congressional offices, to call attention to their blocked opportunities. Their civil disobedience has sometimes resulted in arrests and threats of deportation (Jones, 2010).

The first national Coming Out of the Shadows Week was held in March 2010 and reflects the ways that the urban immigrant youth movement has been inspired by and adopted a major tool of the lesbian, gay, bisexual, transgender, and queer (LGBTQ) rights movement. When undocumented youth "come out," they make their plight visible, reject shame, and confront their fears (Jones, 2010). This strategy also reflects the strong leadership of LGBTQ youth in DREAM organizing, and their identities and struggles that lie at the intersection of immigration status and sexual orientation. Lesbian and gay immigrant youth cannot legalize their status through marriage. They may find the courage to come out as nonheterosexual, yet are still trapped in the closet of their immigration status. Immigrant youth, who are generally less socially and culturally segregated than their parents, appear to be working in coalition with people of other identities and causes more often than older immigrants. This is especially true for partnering on LGBTQ rights issues (Hattam & Yescas, 2010).

Youth activists have appropriated digital media and communication technologies to create new spaces for self-representation and mobilization. Social networking sites, blogs, and websites enable youth to tell their stories and connect with others. Young immigrants also use these tools to provide positive public representations as alternatives to the widespread image of the "illegal immigrant," and to build support and boost visibility for causes including the DREAM Act. Undocumented youths' range of physical movement is limited because of their immigration status and finances. They also face special risks by speaking openly about their status; digital media allows them to network nationally and internationally and express themselves with less peril. The DREAM movement relies heavily on the Internet for sharing youth testimonies and information about the legislative process. Its organizers are committed to training other youth in media and communication skills and strategies (Costanza-Chock, 2010). These technologies are deployed when undocumented youth organize for other political issues, such as fighting deportations of arrested or detained immigrant youth. In 2006, in response to the introduction of the Sensenbrenner bill, Latina/o youth, including the undocumented, used text-messaging and MySpace to communicate and coordinate walkouts throughout the country (Yang, 2007).

Nurturing or Criminalizing Our Future?

In December 2010, after months of immigrant youth mobilizations, the DREAM Act passed in the U.S. House of Representatives for the first time. However, there were not enough Senate votes for the bill to prevent a Republican filibuster. After this failure, youth organizers redirected more attention toward state and local level politics, including blocking punitive legislation and supporting immigrant-friendly bills. In 2011, a variety of DREAM Acts were introduced in states with in-state tuition laws including California, New York, and Illinois. The provisions of these bills vary, but provide a mechanism to raise and distribute private institutional aid to undocumented students. Empowered by their educational and activist accomplishments, immigrant youth appear to be playing more central roles in advocating for these bills than they did in earlier in-state tuition efforts. Although the political landscape is very fluid, in the summer of 2011, the California and Illinois bills were signed into law. Undocumented students are not only fighting for their own educational access; some are traveling to advocate for others. In April 2011, seven undocumented youth, including members of Chicago's Immigrant Youth Justice League, were arrested and jailed in Atlanta. The arrests occurred after they came out as undocumented and delivered a letter to the president of Georgia State University asking him not to comply with a recent ban by the state's Board of Regents on admitting undocumented students to Georgia's top five public universities.

Latina/o immigrant youth are an important demographic who come from varied geographic and social locations and experiences. Their development is critical to the future civic health of the nation, and their activism is dynamic, varied, and differs from that of their elders and their citizen peers. Despite their limited socioeconomic, educational, legal, and political capital and their lower civic engagement by traditional measures, young immigrants may be deeply knowledgeable about and engaged with co-ethnic and immigrant families, communities, and issues. Their participation was especially remarkable in the 2006 immigration protests, the largest demonstrations in U.S history. Youthful immigrants are motivated to improve the lives of those around them because the needs are vast and their parents have sacrificed deeply to offer them better lives. Many retain a sense of community obligation that contrasts with the U.S. celebration of individualism and nuclear family.

Some of the most creative and courageous activism in the United States today is driven by undocumented youth. Despite facing overwhelming obstacles, some are highly involved in bettering their schools and communities, yet their civic engagement patterns are distinctive. Rejected by the nation-state, these young immigrants understand that their life chances and those of their loved ones depend on social change. Immigrant student groups have been organized on college campuses, in high schools, in communities, and online, and serve as incubators for some of the most inventive and dedicated youth leaders in the United States today.

Bilingual and bicultural youth who are transitioning from K-12 inclusion to lives as "illegal" adults exhibit social membership through service to their families, schools, and communities. With state legislative victories that make it more possible for undocumented adolescents to pursue higher education, activism becomes more likely and important for college students who need a pathway to U.S. citizenship to fulfill their potential. Some are engaging in unprecedented actions and protests to change policies at various institutional and government levels. Especially remarkable is their use of youth-driven cultural and communication forums, such as hip-hop and Facebook, and activist forums, such as LGBTQ-inspired "coming out" rallies. Young immigrants demonstrate that they are not an impediment to a healthy democracy; rather, they help to reenergize it. Without passage of laws such as the DREAM Act that will enable undocumented youth who grew up in the United States to fully participate in the nation's civic life, we are in danger of losing many future Latina/o leaders to deportation, depression, and disillusionment.

References

Abrego, L. (2008). Legitimacy, social identity, and the mobilization of law: The effects of Assembly Bill 540 on undocumented students in California. *Law & Social Inquiry*, 33(3), 709–734.

Bada, X., Fox, J., & Selee, A. (Eds.). (2006). *Invisible no more. Mexican migrant civic participation in the United States*. Washington, DC: Woodrow Wilson International Center for Scholars.

Batalova, J., & McHugh, M. (2010). *DREAM vs. reality: An analysis of potential DREAM Act beneficiaries*. Washington, DC: Migration Policy Institute.

Bloemraad, I., & Trost, C. (2008). It's a family affair: Inter-generational mobilization in the spring 2006 protests. *American Behavioral Scientist*, 52(4), 507–532.

Brodkin, K. (2007). *Making democracy matter: Identity and activism in Los Angeles*. New Brunswick, NJ: Rutgers University Press.

Costanza-Chock, S. (2010). *Se ve, se siente: Transmedia mobilization in the Los Angeles immigrants rights movement*. Los Angeles, CA: University of Southern California, Los Angeles.

Flores-González, N. (2010). Immigrants, citizens or both?: The second generation in the immigrant rights marches. In A. Pallares & N. Flores-González (Eds.), *¡Marcha! Latino Chicago and the immigrant rights movement*. Champaign, IL: University of Illinois Press.

Gonzales, R. G. (2008). Left out but not shut down: Political activism and the undocumented Latino student movement. *Northwestern Journal of Law and Social Policy*, 3(2), 219–239.

Hattam, V., & Yescas, C. (2010). From immigration and race to sex and faith: Reimagining the politics of opposition. *Social Research*, 77(1), 133–162.

Jones, M. (2010, October 21). Coming out illegal. *New York Times*, p. MM36.

Lopez, M. H., & Marcelo, K. B. (2008). The civic engagement of immigrant youth: New evidence from the 2006 Civic and Political Health of the Nation Survey. *Applied Developmental Science, 12*(2), 66–73.

Madera, G. (Ed.). (2008). *Underground undergrads: UCLA undocumented immigrant students speak out*. Los Angeles, CA: UCLA Center for Labor Research and Education.

Marcelo, K. B., & Lopez, M. H. (2006). *Immigrant youth demographics*. Medford/Somerville, MA: The Center for Information and Research on Civic Learning and Engagement, Tufts University.

Marcelo, K. B., Lopez, M. H., & Kirby, E. H. (2007). *Civic engagement among minority youth*. Medford/Somerville, MA: The Center for Information and Research on Civic Learning and Engagement, Tufts University.

Migration Policy Institute. (2010). *MPI updates national and state-level estimates of potential DREAM act beneficiaries*. Washington, DC: Author.

National Immigration Law Center. (2010). Pro-DREAM activity shows that the immigration movement is stronger than ever. Retrieved from http://www.nilc.org /immlawpolicy/dream/Summary-of-DREAM-Activities-2010-12-15.pdf.

Passel, J. S. (2011). Demography of immigrant youth: Past, present, and future. *Future of Children, 21*(1), 19–41.

Passel, J. S., Cohn, D., & Hugo Lopez, M. (2011). Hispanics account for more than half of nation's growth in past decade. Washington, DC: Pew Hispanic Center.

Pérez Huber, L. (2010). *Sueños indocumentados: Using LatCrit to explore the testimonios of undocumented and U.S. born Chicana college students on discourses of racist nativism in education* (Unpublished doctoral dissertation). University of California, Los Angeles.

Perez, W., Espinoza, R., Ramos, K., Coronado, H., & Cortés, R. (2009). Academic resilience among undocumented Latino students. *Hispanic Journal of Behavioral Sciences, 31*, 149–181.

Perez, W., Espinoza, R., Ramos, K., Coronado, H., & Cortés, R. D. (2010). Civic engagement patterns of undocumented Mexican students. *Journal of Hispanic Higher Education, 9*, 245–265.

Perla, H., Jr. (2010). Monseñor Romero's resurrection: Transnational Salvadoran organizing. *NACLA Report on the Americas, 43*(6), 25–31.

Plyler v. Doe, 457 U.S. 202 (1982).

Portes, A., & Bach, R. (1985). *Latin journey: Cuban and Mexican immigrants in the United States*. Berkeley, CA: University of California Press.

Reich, G., & Mendoza, A. A. (2008). "Educating kids" versus "coddling criminals": Framing the debate over instate tuition for undocumented students in Kansas. *State Politics and Policy Quarterly, 8*(2), 177–197.

Reynolds, J., & Orellana, M. F. (2009). New immigrant youth interpreting in white public space. *American Anthropologist, 111*(2), 211–223.

Rincón, A. (2008). *Undocumented immigrants and higher education: Si se puede!* New York, NY: LFB Scholarly Publishing.

Rogers, J., Saunders, M., Terriquez, V., & Velez, V. (2008). Civic lessons, public schools, and the civic development of undocumented students and parents. *Northwestern Journal of Law and Social Policy, 3*, 201–218.

Sanders, M. S. (2010). Hope, opportunity, and access: The in-state tuition debate in North Carolina. *Journal of Latinos and Education, 9*(2), 108–125.

Seif, H. (2004). "'Wise up!' Undocumented Latino youth, Mexican-American legislators, and the struggle for higher education. *Latino Studies, 2*, 210–230.

Seif, H. (2010). The civic life of Latina/o immigrant youth: Challenging boundaries and creating safe spaces. In L. R. Sherrod, J. Torney-Purta, & C. A. Flanagan (Eds.), *Handbook of research on civic engagement in youth* (p. 445). Hoboken, NJ: Wiley.

S.I.N. Collective. (2007). Students Informing Now (S.I.N.) challenge the racial state in California without shame . . .'SIN vergüenza!' *Educational Foundations, 21*(1–2), 71–90.

Stepick, A., Dutton Stepick, C., & Labissiere, C. Y. (2008). South Florida's immigrant youth and civic engagement: Major engagement: Minor differences. *Applied Developmental Science, 12*(2), 57–65.

Torney-Purta, J., Barber, C., & Wilkenfeld, B. (2006). Differences in the civic knowledge and attitudes of adolescents in the United States by immigrant status and Hispanic background. *Prospects: Quarterly Review of Comparative Education, 36*(3), 343–354.

Valenzuela, A. (1999). *Subtractive schooling: U.S.-Mexican youth and the politics of caring.* Albany, NY: State University of New York Press.

Yang, K. W. (2007). Organizing MySpace: Youth, walkouts, pleasure, politics, and new media. *Educational Foundations, 21*, 9–28.

HINDA SEIF is assistant professor of anthropology and women/gender studies at the University of Illinois at Springfield. E-mail: hseif2@uis.edu

Serpell, R., Mumba, P., & Chansa-Kabali, T. (2011). Early educational foundations for the development of civic responsibility: An African experience. In C. A. Flanagan & B. D. Christens (Eds.), Youth civic development: Work at the cutting edge. *New Directions for Child and Adolescent Development, 134*, 77–93.

6

Early Educational Foundations for the Development of Civic Responsibility: An African Experience

Robert Serpell, Paul Mumba, Tamara Chansa-Kabali

Abstract

An innovative curriculum designed to foster the development of social responsibility among pre-adolescent children was introduced at a rural Zambian primary school. The curriculum invoked Child-to-Child principles focusing on health education, advancing a synthesis of Western psychological theories and African cultural traditions. The teacher sought to democratize the educational process through cooperative learning in mixed-gender, mixed-social-class, and mixed-ability study groups. Learners engaged in community service activities and contributed to the nurturant care of younger children. Young adults interviewed seventeen years after completing the program recalled their experience and reflected on how it had promoted their personal agency, cooperative disposition, and civic responsibility in early adulthood. © 2011 Wiley Periodicals, Inc.

This chapter builds on an earlier presentation by Serpell and Chansa-Kabali (2010).

NEW DIRECTIONS FOR CHILD AND ADOLESCENT DEVELOPMENT, no. 134, Winter 2011 © Wiley Periodicals, Inc.
Published online in Wiley Online Library (wileyonlinelibrary.com). • DOI: 10.1002/cd.312

Civic responsibility emerges in youth and adulthood from an individual's experiences earlier in life in various social contexts, structured by family socialization processes, by peer relations, and in many cases by schooling. In this chapter, we examine the influence on youth civic development of an innovative school curriculum designed to foster the development of responsibility among pre-adolescent children in a predominantly rural region of Africa. In the next section, Robert Serpell explains the theoretical grounding in developmental, educational and cultural psychology for the innovative curriculum observed at Kabale, a government primary school in the small Zambian town of Mpika. Then the origins, rationale, and practices of the curriculum are presented by Paul Mumba, one of the teachers who pioneered its development in the 1990s. A major source of inspiration for the innovations he describes was the Child-to-Child (CtC) approach, originally conceptualized in the 1980s by an international consortium coordinated by London University's Institute of Education. Then, Tamara Chansa-Kabali and Robert Serpell reflect on what they have learned so far from an ongoing study that invites graduates of the Kabale CtC curriculum, now in their late twenties, to look back and interpret the significance of their pre-adolescent experiences at school in forming their current outlook on society and their adult responsibilities. Finally, in the last section we offer an integrative interpretation of the significance of the Kabale experience for the promotion of civic responsibility in Zambia and other societies facing similar challenges in the twenty-first century.

The situation of the youth in Zambia in 2011 is fraught with adversities, including severely limited educational opportunities beyond the first seven years of basic education, very few openings in the formal sector of the economy for those with less than tertiary-level educational certificates, and a devastatingly high prevalence of human immunodeficiency virus (HIV) and acquired immunodeficiency syndrome (AIDS), especially among the sexually active youth. "Despite international development advocacy for young persons' rights and abilities, like many other national governments, that of Zambia continues to depict young people in ways that leave little scope to acknowledge their agency. One way is the welfare angle that treats young people as dependent and immature, and therefore in need of 'improvement.' Another is problem-oriented and characterizes young people as troublesome and therefore prone to problematic behavior that needs controlling and curtailing . . ." (Hansen, 2008, p. 213). In the present chapter, we document the perspective of a group of Zambian youth in their late twenties who believe that their experience in pre-adolescent childhood at primary school prepared them well to cope with adversity in ways that are neither dependent nor troublesome, by offering them opportunities to learn through active participation their responsibility to reach out and contribute cooperatively to the well-being of their community.

NEW DIRECTIONS FOR CHILD AND ADOLESCENT DEVELOPMENT • DOI: 10.1002/cd

Theoretical Grounding in Developmental, Educational, and Cultural Psychology

The research program on which this chapter is based is framed within Robert Serpell's cultural perspective on applied developmental psychology that conceptualizes education as facilitating the appropriation of new ideas by learners through participating in socially organized activities (Serpell, 2008). Rather than conceiving instruction as the "de-contextualized" transmission of information, this perspective on education emphasizes the benefits of situating learning opportunities within the sociocultural context in which the target student activity will be applied in everyday life.

The pedagogical practices of institutionalized public basic schooling (IPBS), a model that has become increasingly standardized across the world in the late twentieth century, stand in marked contrast to the traditional family socialization practices and beliefs of many African societies. IPBS tends to emphasize "advance preparation as against on-the-spot assistance," and "authorised competence as against practical competence" (Serpell & Hatano, 1997, pp. 367–368). The Western cultural origins of this model are traceable in Zambia to a process of hegemonic imposition by Christian missionaries from Europe in the nineteenth and early twentieth centuries in the name of evangelization, and further entrenched by a colonial administration that shared with the missions assumptions of European cultural superiority and a view of African cultures as devoid of ideas relevant to the design of education. The racist connotations of those assumptions came under critical attack in the decolonization movement as incompatible with the egalitarian ideals of modern thought enshrined in the United Nations Declaration of Universal Human Rights. Yet, paradoxically, the essential character of the IPBS model has been preserved in many independent African nations, along with a number of extrinsic features, some of which are culturally problematic, as we explain below.

The indigenous cultures of Zambia and other African societies exhibit patterns of social organization and principles of moral evaluation some of which resemble closely those embedded in the indigenous cultures of Europe, while others are markedly different. A study of conceptions of intelligence among the Chewa people in a rural community of Eastern Zambia (Serpell, 1993a, 1996) found that adults explaining their reasons for assigning important responsibilities to children they knew well in the village invoked a concept, -nzelu, that includes connotations of wisdom, intelligence, cleverness, and skill, but places greater emphasis than the English concept of intelligence on a dimension of social responsibility (-tumukila). On the other hand, when describing children who performed well at school they were more likely to invoke the concept of -chenjela (cleverness or cognitive alacrity). To qualify for the designation of -nzelu, an individual must display both the qualities -*chenjela* and -*tumukila*. Moreover a person who is -*chenjela*, but not -*tumikila* is regarded as socially dangerous.

Similar conceptions of intelligence have been documented for several other African cultures, including the Baoule culture of Cote d'Ivoire (Dasen et al., 1985), the Luo culture of Kenya (Grigorenko et al., 2001), and the Bemba culture of Northern Zambia (Kingsley, 1985). A widespread African child-rearing practice that relates directly to the cultivation of social responsibility is that of sending young children on errands. Ogunnaike and Houser (2002) report that Yoruba mothers selling goods at the city market in Nigeria started doing this with children as young as three years old, as indeed do rural Chewa parents in Zambia (Serpell, 1993a) and Kikuyu parents in rural Kenya (Levine & Levine, 1963). Nsamenang (1992) refers to this practice as a form of social priming, designed to prepare young children for real domestic tasks that will be assigned to them when they grow a little older. It is noteworthy that in the Chewa language the root of the word for social responsibility (-*tumikila*) is -*tuma*, meaning to send.

In rural African societies, children were traditionally raised to believe that they were brought up by the community, that they were part of the community, and that in due course they would play an important role in the development of the community. Implementation of the IPBS model in rural African neighborhoods has often seemed to be quite alien to the community whose children it recruits. A longitudinal trace of the life-journeys of young people born into the rural Chewa community that hosted the study of -*nzelu* cited above found that only a minority of them (and none of the girls) completed the full seven-year primary course, even though there were plenty of places at the local school (Serpell, 1993a). Reasons for dropping out were manifold, but the most common explanation offered by the young people themselves was that they lacked sufficient -*nzelu* to cope with the curriculum. Yet many of them were ostensibly competent to cope with the demands of adult life, suggesting that the problem arose from an inappropriate school curriculum rather than lack of individual intelligence. Furthermore, both parents and teachers expected that very few of those who completed the course and qualified for a place in eighth grade would return to live in the neighborhood and contribute to its economy. Thus, the paradigm of schooling included an extractive definition of academic success. Critical analysis of this situation generated a call for greater local accountability by primary schools to the local rural communities they purport to serve (Serpell, 1999b).

The activities of the Child-to-Child curriculum observed at Kabale school in the 1990s included a number of distinctive features that respond to this challenge (Serpell, 2008). One of these was a cross-cutting theme of monitoring the growth of young children in the first five years of life. In many African countries, including Zambia, the public health system distributes to the parents of young children a record card on which the child's weight is entered as a point on a printed growth chart that situates the child's actual weight relative to statistical norms (Morley & Woodland, 1988). The card is kept at home by the child's family and brought at each visit to a clinic for periodic updating, so that cumulatively a graph displays whether this individual is within the normal range for his or her age, and whether he or she is growing steadily over time. Kabale students in fifth to seventh grades were assigned to find one of these growth charts in use for a sibling at home or a neighbor's child, to escort the child to the clinic, with or in place of a parent, to watch how the record is entered, and to interpret the significance of the graph for that child's healthy development.

Building on the interpretation of the growth chart, students at Kabale learned about the nutritional care of young children, including oral rehydration with a homemade solution of sugar and salt during episodes of diarrhea. Nurturant care of younger children served as a productive contribution to the life of the student's family and/or other families in the local community, and as a priming for the student's development of skills and attitudes expected of him or her in adulthood. Project work both in the classroom and outside was organized in study teams, which served as an opportunity for cooperative learning in which students co-constructed solutions to problems assigned by the teacher, and thus raised their awareness of the complementarity of individual talents, the potential cognitive synergies of collaboration, and the socioemotional challenges of negotiating roles within a group. Thus in terms of developmental theory, the CtC curriculum at Kabale included theoretically powerful affordances for the development of personal competencies and dispositions conducive to civic responsibility.

Barbara Rogoff (1993) has proposed that developmental change occurs over time on three complementary planes. Participatory appropriation is "the process by which individuals transform their understanding of and responsibility for activities through their own participation" (p. 150). Guided participation refers to an arrangement between people that facilitates appropriation. And apprenticeship is a "system of interpersonal involvements and arrangements in which people engage in culturally organized activity in which apprentices become more responsible participants" (p. 144). The CtC curriculum at Kabale Primary School can be seen as an apprenticeship system, through which the teacher guided the participation of the children in activities in such a way that their understanding of and responsibility for those activities was transformed. In the follow-up study we explore just how radical and how lasting that transformation was.

The history of how CtC achieved prominence in the Zambian public school system in the 1990s has been traced by Udell (2001), and a case study by a research team at the University of Zambia has documented the short-term impact of its exemplary implementation in Mpika (a small town in Zambia's predominantly Bemba-speaking northern province), in

NEW DIRECTIONS FOR CHILD AND ADOLESCENT DEVELOPMENT • DOI: 10.1002/cd

terms of students' practical knowledge of preventive health, their academic achievement, and their parents' appreciation of the curriculum (Mwape & Serpell, 1996; Serpell, 2008; Serpell & Mwape, 1998/99). The following retrospective account of its rationale was written by Paul Mumba, one of the leading teachers involved in development of the CtC approach in Zambia.

Paul Mumba's Account of His Educational Innovation at Kabale Primary School, Mpika, Zambia, 1995–1997

Child-to-Child: An Empowering Approach to Health Promotion. CtC is a broadly conceptualized approach to the integration of education and health with the aim of realizing the potential of the children as agents of preventive health in their schools, their homes, and communities. According to Pridmore (1999, p. 15), CtC rests upon the beliefs that "children learn health messages and pass them on to siblings, peers, parents and their community; learning should be active and fun; children can be partners with adults to improve health, and health and education should work together" (see the Child-to-Child Trust website for more details; http://www.child-to-child.org).

In Zambia CtC was officially launched by the then head of state, Kenneth Kaunda. In his speech, he urged the introduction of CtC as a way of promoting health countrywide and challenged all children to regard themselves as fighters for health. Through CtC activities, children are given the opportunity to provide much needed linkages between the school and the home/community. The concept of CtC has been used to help develop children's full participation and potential not only in the classroom and the school but also in the communities. A major theme of CtC is that as children grow, they should become responsible citizens not only in their families but also in their communities. CtC avoids the dysfunctional separation of IPBS from everyday life by ensuring that not only literacy, but also skills and attitudes for real life are taught intensively in schools. If young people are taught early in life about the significance of family planning and spacing, taking children to under-five clinics, and voting, even if they do not complete a full twelve-year program of education, they will be equipped to exercise their responsibilities for participation in national development.

In 1994–1995, the United Nations Children's Fund (UNICEF) distributed to every teacher countrywide the major resource book by Hawes and Scotchmer (1993, p. 14), which contained facts and ideas for health promotion in schools; it was this book that helped me to understand the concept of health. Health was defined as a "healthy environment, being fit and well, healthy mind, healthy relationship and helping others." I was led to understand that it was not just the absence of diseases as perceived by many people including the well informed. This definition of health led me to design a way of learning building upon the CtC approach that would contribute to solving the challenges I had been experiencing in my teaching responsibilities. Through constant reflection on the activities with the children the following practices were initiated in the classes.

Cooperative Learning. To create happy relations and a good environment, I initiated cooperative learning and group work, which was different from the usual groups implemented in most public schools. Many Bemba proverbs point to the principle of interdependence and the reciprocal benefits of cooperation (e.g. "One finger can't pick a louse"; "You don't have eyes in the back of your head"; "Whom will you ask if you are alone?"), as do many Bemba traditional practices. Setting up cooperative study groups that included both girls and boys was a strategy to close the gaps created by their cultural background in a school setting. I had observed that girls tended to associate themselves with other girls and separated themselves from the boys. In addition to seeking ways of eliminating gender differences in academic performance, an important factor motivating my decision to set up mixed-gender study groups was thinking ahead to what would make the students better wives or husbands when they grew up. Later, when the study groups were established, participating students began to question the cultural conventions that used to keep male and female students apart.

Reflecting on the need for group goals and individual accountability, I introduced children to evaluating their own performance as a group. Then, the groups in the class would be compared to find the group that had done well, and this was held up as evidence of being cooperative. This caused concern among faster learners who did not want their groups to be associated with failure; as a result they were persuaded to help out slow learners on their own time and in their own homes so as to improve the performance of their groups (Mumba, 1995).

Some teachers have argued that this method takes too long and are reluctant to attempt it because they are keen to march ahead with the syllabus. My opinion from observation is that, once children are trained, the operations become easier and faster. I divided the class into groups. These groups were of mixed ability and sex. Each group comprised six pupils. Two pupils represented the group as leaders and both sexes were represented in the leadership. I thus implemented the chain of responsibility for assisting that Tharp and Gallimore (1988) developed in their research building on the ideas of Vygotsky's (1978) zone of proximal development. This meant that I had to help the group leaders discover how to help other pupils participate in their own learning. The group leaders specified the following roles for themselves:

- Ensure that each pupil had the required material to use in the classroom such as pencils and exercise books and possibly the group would help those that were lacking.

- Ensure that members were neat in writing. Encourage corrections before any new work.
- Evaluate their group's performance and discuss problems in the group.
- Keep and write end of day report for the teacher to evaluate his or her work.
- Represent the group in the academic meetings with the teacher.
- Suggest other new ways of learning in consultation with other members according to their needs.
- Monitor late coming and ensure that latecomers were paired with responsible pupils for encouragement.
- Monitor absenteeism in groups. They were to visit pupils that were often absent from school.

Democratization of the Classroom. My interest in democratization in the classroom was partly inspired by the question: "What causes riots in schools?" It seems that many youth participating in school riots perceive them as "the shortest route to being heard." This implies a criticism of the school authorities for not offering students other, less dangerous, alternative avenues to make their voices heard. Another motivating concern was the frequency of strike action in industry, which prompted me to ask, "What is the role of psychology in preventing industrial unrest?" I was interested in the process through which union leaders, elected as activists, often discover through access to company documents that there are real constraints on what management can do to address workers' demands, but when they try to share this discovery with the members who elected them, they are rejected as "sell-outs." I believe that freedom of expression needs to be constrained by responsibility, and this is something that can be taught in school.

To democratize the class I had to create awareness of rights among the children. This was a difficult component to implement. CtC seeks to promote this element of liberating children to participate actively in the learning process, but many teachers criticized this approach, arguing that creating awareness in children about their rights may promote misbehavior. In my opinion, this is debatable. The children in my class were exposed to their rights as documented in the United Nations Convention on the Rights of the Child. This was done through class discussions in their Spiritual and Moral Education Studies lessons (part of the national curriculum introduced in the 1990s to replace religious studies). What children discovered was that each right had responsibilities that went along with it. I guided them to more discussion of their responsibilities as can be seen from these two examples:

1. Right to education: "Work hard at school"—"Avoid absenteeism"— "Go to school early"
2. Right to recreation (play): "Plan time to play"—"Choose good friends"

NEW DIRECTIONS FOR CHILD AND ADOLESCENT DEVELOPMENT • DOI: 10.1002/cd

Several rights were discussed and the class survey revealed that they enjoyed most the "right to speak freely and voice own opinions." Although most teachers interviewed supported this right, some were reluctant to include it in their actual classes, arguing that it conflicts with indigenous Zambian tradition. For instance, one Bemba proverb prohibits children from speaking openly in the presence of their elders. Our cultural norms, on the other hand, do allow a child to argue with or criticize his or her peers because this is the wisest thing to do, but an argument with an adult is not a sign of respect. This is the background from which our teachers and pupils are coming. When pupils were asked to narrate reasons why they enjoyed the right to speak freely and voice their own opinions in their classroom, they responded as follows:

"We are able to argue and defend our views."
"We are able to ask freely."
"It builds our confidence."
"We are able to contribute."
"We are able to express our problems."
"We are able to challenge bullies and other people that oppress us."
"It removes shyness." (Most girls expressed this.)
"Get ideas from peers."

For further details of the implications of CtC for democratization in the classroom, see Mumba (2000).

Social Responsibility. The CtC approach seeks to cultivate nurturance, cooperation, social responsibility, self-confidence, practical problem solving, and healthy life styles. One activity through which the curriculum attempted to cultivate these psychosocial attributes was assigning children to monitor the growth of younger siblings in the community. I introduced children to maintaining growth charts for their younger siblings or other younger children in the community when these children reach the age of two and a half years. This is the age at which many rural Zambian parents stop bringing their children to the clinic for weighing, focusing their attention, instead, on the next child to be born. This responsibility was then taken on by children involved in the CtC program. Providing children with the opportunity to participate in the care of a younger child has potential educational value as an opportunity to cultivate nurturant responsibility, a moral quality relatively neglected in the curriculum of most contemporary public school systems. I see the CtC outreach health activities of our primary school students as laying the foundations for intersectoral collaboration between health and education, provoking the breakdown of professional and administrative barriers between the sectors. In this way, even when my students were still young they were actively engaged in civic reform, expanding the awareness of teachers and health workers of how they can better serve the public by integrating their complementary fields of endeavor.

Developmental Outcomes and Adult Recollections of Former CtC Pupils

More recently, two of us, Tamara Chansa-Kabali and Robert Serpell, embarked on a long-term follow-up study of young women and men, now in their late twenties, who were enrolled in the program at Kabale in the 1990s and some of their local contemporaries enrolled in the conventional curriculum at the same school. The goal has been to explore through qualitative analysis of in-depth interviews the longer-term psychological consequences of engagement in CtC activities from fifth to seventh grade. The informants interviewed to date include some whose formal education ended with seventh grade while others went on from secondary to tertiary education and are now embarking on a professional career (including a nurse, two teachers, a religious pastor, a diplomate in journalism, and a diplomate in social work).

We have been struck by the difference of focus and intensity between the recollection and opinions voiced by respondents who were enrolled in a CtC class and those whose teachers at Kabale used conventional pedagogical practices. The latter group remembers mostly sports and clubs. Those who were enrolled in a CtC class, on the other hand, recalled with remarkable consistency several of the themes discussed in the above section, often relating these to abstract philosophical principles that had made an enduring impact on their later lives.

As Fivush, Bohanek, and Zaman (2011) have shown, in middle-class American culture, "individual narrative selves are created within families and across generations" (p. 45), mediated by recurrent activities such as family dinner conversations, with young people invoking their parents' stories as resources for interpreting their own life-journeys. Many of the young Zambians we have interviewed seem to have created narrative selves through peer-group-mediated conversations about their shared CtC experiences at Kabale school. At the end of the interview guide for our study, the following questions were asked of each respondent: "What are the things that you have carried on as an adult from your experiences at Kabale? How have the experiences at Kabale contributed to your life today?" Most of the former students of Paul Mumba's CtC class at Kabale responded to these questions with enthusiasm, attributing both concrete practices of their current adult lives and abstract principles informing those practices to enduring themes appropriated through formative experiences in their upper primary school years.

Peer-Group Cooperation, Gender Equality, and Helping Others. *Group Work, Group Learning.* Several respondents spoke passionately about their study groups, expressing a sense of enduring group solidarity and referring to their former classmates in the same group as "my member." One of the values pervading group work was that of encouraging slow learners. As one respondent testified: "We used to be in groups, it was very encouraging. I was not good at school work: I got encouraged because at least I had someone by my side to help, and we really had that true spirit in the classroom and everybody was helped . . . We played together, did everything together . . . we lived like a team!" (23)[1]

A female primary school teacher had internalized this as a pedagogical principle in her own professional work: "I've learned that you can get help from anybody . . . no one is dull . . . interacting with others, mingling, making friends." (6)

For several respondents the impact of this aspect of the CtC curriculum had been to generate a broader, prosocial disposition to help others, to share knowledge, and to cooperate in social projects. Other responses to the question "What are the things that you have carried on as an adult . . .?" included:

"Having a heart for other people." (2)

"I've learned to respect other people; to live in a group; to control myself spiritually." (24)

"Working together, because you know unity is the key to success; you are able to express yourself." (9)

"To be free, to associate with people 'cos without people you can't live alone of course." (10)

"This time I come to realize how important Mr. Mumba was, because I am applying the life skills he had oriented me to at that moment." (44)

"Maybe it helped me very much being confident in myself. That's what I got from Kabale Primary School that has helped me very much today." (3)

One of the respondents recalled Kabale School as "a beautiful place, full of activities." These activities, steered by their teacher, were embraced by the families and parents and the entire community. The activities conducted by the children in the community brought cleanliness and sanitation to the school and home environments. The study groups were mixed, including some students who came from higher social class homes and others from very poor homes. Despite those differences in socioeconomic status, the children worked together as one family. For instance, one reported that they would go to the extent of donating some money for someone in the group who did not have washing soap at home for cleaning his uniform. They also took turns to conduct their group work from home to home regardless of status.

Gender Equality, Mixed Coed Study Groups. With regard to gender differentiation of roles in class activities, a respondent from the non-CtC group recalled that there were differences especially when it came to sweeping—that boys were not as smart at this task because that was not their role and therefore girls would take it up and make sure that the classroom looked smart. In contrast, a former CtC student revealed that even though such gender differences existed initially, they disappeared as time went by. She recalled a seminal occasion when the teacher, who was male, showed the boys an example: he swept and cleaned the classroom by himself. This exemplary demonstration put an end to the belief by the boys and girls that they should have different roles depending on their gender. A female respondent recalled: "I would say there was no difference between boys and girls in the class because even us girls we would want to reach the boys' level, so we worked a lot—there was no difference . . . And like today life, and when I went to college, I had to meet men now in our class, it was not very difficult for me to interact . . . it helped me very much being confident in myself." (3)

One male respondent quipped: "We saw our girl classmates as sisters, not as wives," seeming to imply that egalitarian relations between the sexes have no place within a marriage. But later in the same interview this respondent, reflecting on his own adult family life, emphasized his willingness to handle domestic chores at home and proudly affirmed that he had an egalitarian relationship with his wife. (27)

Health Care Practices, Personal Hygiene, Environmental Care. These key curriculum objectives were widely cited by our informants, many of whom attested that the habits instilled in them at Primary School had remained with them in later life. This may not be a unique feature of the CtC curriculum because Hoppers (1981) and others have documented a preoccupation with personal cleanliness as a distinctive characteristic of many primary school leavers in Zambia, and LeVine, LeVine, Richman, Uribe, and Correa (1994) have shown that in several countries with low rates of school enrollment the infants of mothers with complete primary schooling have reliably better prospects of survival and health. However, some of the narratives provided by our respondents afford striking evidence of direct causal connections that serve to put some flesh on the correlational literature. For instance, several of the young parents in our sample, including fathers, went out of their way to assert that they take their under-five child regularly to the well-baby clinic for check-ups. In a striking case reported elsewhere (Serpell, 2001), a young mother whose formal credentials at the end of seventh grade were such that she did not qualify for a place in eighth grade described in convincing detail how she had shared with another young mother skills and understanding rooted in modern biomedical science that enabled her to save an infant's life.

Contrasts Between CtC at Kabale and the Pedagogical Practices of High Schools. According to the recollections of respondents who continued their schooling beyond seventh grade, the practice of assigning learners to study in groups in the CtC classes at Kabale was unique. Indeed, several of them recalled that they were explicitly told by their teachers in high school that they should work as individuals. Yet it was

NEW DIRECTIONS FOR CHILD AND ADOLESCENT DEVELOPMENT • DOI: 10.1002/cd

clear to many of them, based on their CtC experience at Kabale, that coop-erative problem solving was a valuable strategy for educational settings, which some of them adopted on their own initiative.

With few exceptions, the respondents confirmed the findings of the earlier case study conducted while this cohort was still enrolled at Kabale. Most of them recalled that their parents encouraged their participation in the CtC because they knew that the experiences they were going through would be relevant for them in the future. Several of the former CtC stu-dents considered the nature of their primary education to have been sig-nificantly different from that of contemporary Zambian schools, and expressed sadness that the education they went through, which was bene-ficial to their present lives was not currently practiced in the schools.

For some of our respondents who did not go on to tertiary education the long-term benefits of group work in upper primary school included a lasting respect for individuals of lesser academic aptitude as having other complementary strengths, another important resource for adult citizenship.

Agency and Responsibility in Adolescence and Early Adulthood

The CtC approach adopted by Paul Mumba and his colleagues at Kabale Primary School evidently made a profound impact on many of his stu-dents. Fourteen years later, they remembered vividly the study group orga-nization of the class as exciting and empowering. They also retained a clear memory of the philosophical themes of helping others, cooperative learning, and gender equality. Many of those who went on to further edu-cation regarded the CtC approach as superior to the more individualistic educational practices they encountered elsewhere. Although this evalua-tion may reflect the emphasis on collectivist values of traditional African culture, it is clear that the experience of CtC added something important to their home socialization because these values did not feature in our interviews with youths who had attended the same school, but were enrolled in classes that did not adopt the CtC approach.

Several key features of the approach stand out for us as having given this cohort of young people an important sense of personal agency condu-cive to civic participation later in life. The assignment of genuine respon-sibilities to them at an early age for reaching out to intervene in the wider community, with an emphasis on nurturance of the development of chil-dren younger than themselves, seems to have cultivated in many of them an enduring prosocial disposition to help others in need. The pressure to cooperate in mixed-gender, mixed-social-class, and mixed-ability study groups seems to have heightened their awareness of social interdepen-dency and laid the foundations for egalitarian relations with members of the opposite sex. The requirement to express their own opinions verbally opened their minds to the values of reasoning and debate that are central to democracy in a knowledge society.

On a theoretical level, participation in the completion and interpretation of the growth chart introduces children to the technology of health science as mobilizing socially distributed cognition (Salomon, 1993), such that when a child is weighed at the under-five clinic, the growth chart printed on the record card, the family escort, and the health professional each contribute complementary information for determining the health and nutritional status of the child. Viewed from this perspective, the cognitive possibilities afforded by the technology are mediated by co-constructive processes among participants in a socially organized activity (Valsiner, 1991). The developmental context of such activities comprises not only a behavioral system of relationships (Bronfenbrenner, 1979), but also a representational system of meanings (D'Andrade, 1984; Sameroff & Fiese, 1992). The representational character of the meanings woven into the sociocultural context "makes it clear that the system is open to deliberate change by its participants, albeit only gradually, and often with great difficulty" (Serpell, 1999a, pp. 42–43). Acknowledging the mutually constitutive relationship between culture and cognition (Cole, 1985) provides a basis for recruiting the imaginative creativity of young learners in the appropriation of a dynamically evolving cultural system of meanings rather than treating them as passive recipients of fossilized knowledge (Serpell, 1993b). The CtC curriculum at Kabale explicitly invited students not only to continue a traditional pattern of responsible participation in family life by caring for younger siblings, but also to expand it to include boys as well as girls, and to critique traditional attitudes and practices inconsistent with modern science.

Although most Zambian families have responded positively to the expansion of formal basic schooling in recent decades by enrolling their children, this does not guarantee that their children will be able to face and solve the challenges they will encounter later in real life. In our view, teachers and curriculum developers should have a broader vision for education, beyond imparting the skills of reading, writing, and mathematics. Children need to be integrated at an appropriate level to participate in civic development. The concept of CtC declined in political visibility in Zambia in the late 1990s, upstaged by other programmatic themes such as promotion of girls' education, poverty reduction, and the fight against HIV and AIDS. Yet, as a philosophical approach, rather than a program, it appears to us to have enduring relevance. Moreover, the particular emphasis at Kabale on engagement by preadolescent children in the nurturant care of younger children seems to have been a uniquely powerful theme for instantiating the approach.

Some commentators in the field of international advocacy for children's rights have argued that the responsibility for taking children to

NEW DIRECTIONS FOR CHILD AND ADOLESCENT DEVELOPMENT • DOI: 10.1002/cd

under-five clinics is too heavy for a primary school age child, but this is part of everyday life for most children in Africa, who are expected to care for their younger siblings. In African tradition, a child who is above the age of eight is seen as someone who can take on certain responsibilities. It is only when they arrive at school that we hear some people objecting that this is a form of child labor. Rather than a form of exploitation, we suggest that the mobilization in CtC of this traditional socialization practice has served to embed early experience of taking responsibility within school education, thus reducing its alienating effects and cultivating a sense of personal and social agency, an essential foundation for effective civic participation later in life.

References

Bronfenbrenner, U. (1979). *The ecology of human development*. Cambridge, MA: Harvard University Press.

Cole, M. (1985). The zone of proximal development: where culture and cognition create each other. In J. V. Wertsch (Ed.), *Culture, communication and cognition: Vygotskian perspectives* (pp. 146–61). Cambridge, England: Cambridge University Press.

D'Andrade, R. (1984). Cultural meaning systems. In R. A. Shweder & R. Levine (Eds.), *Culture theory: Essays on mind, self and emotion*. Cambridge, England: Cambridge University Press.

Dasen, P. R., Barthelemy, D., Kan, E., Kouame, Â. K., Daouda, K., Adjei, K. K., & Assande, Â. N. (1985). N'glouele, l'intelligence chez les Baoule. [Intelligence among the Baoule]. *Archives de Psychologie, 53*, 295–324.

Fivush, R., Bohanek, J. G., & Zaman, W. (2011). Personal and intergenerational narratives in relation to adolescents' well-being. In T. Habermas (Ed.), The development of autobiographical reasoning in adolescence and beyond. *New Directions in Child and Adolescent Development, 131*, 45–57.

Grigorenko, E. L., Geissler, P. W., Prince, R., Okatcha, F., Nokes, C., & Kenny, D. A. (2001). The organisation of Luo conceptions of intelligence: A study of implicit theories in a Kenyan. *International Journal of Behavioral Development, 25*, 367–378.

Hansen, K. (2008). Conclusion: Urban youth in a global world. In K. T. Hansen, A. L. Dahlsgaard, K. V. Gough, U. A. Madsen, K. Valentin, & N. Wildermuth (Eds.), *Youth and the city in the global south* (pp. 207–220). Bloomington, IN: Indiana University Press.

Hawes, H., & Scotchmer C. (Eds.). (1993). *Children for health*. London, England: The Child-to-Child Trust, UNICEF.

Hoppers, W. (1981). *Education in a rural society: Primary pupils and school leavers in Mwinilunga, Zambia*. Lusaka, Zambia: Institute for African Studies.

Kingsley, P. R. (1985). Rural Zambian values and attitudes concerning cognitive competence. In I. R. Lagunes & Y. H. Poortinga (Eds.), *From a different perspective: Studies of behaviour across cultures* (pp. 281–303). Lisse, The Netherlands: Swets & Zeitlinger.

LeVine, R., & Levine, B. (1963). Nyansongo. In B. B. Whiting (Ed.), *Six cultures: Studies of child-rearing* (pp. 15–202). New York, NY: Wiley.

LeVine, R., LeVine, S., Richman, A., Uribe, F., & Correa, C. (1994). Schooling and survival: The impact of maternal education on health and reproduction in the third world. In L. Chen, A. Kleinman, & N. Ware (Eds.), *Health and social change in international perspective* (pp. 303–338). Boston, MA: Harvard Press.

Morley, D., & Woodland, M. (1988). *See how they grow: Monitoring child growth for appropriate health care in developing countries.* London, England: MacMillan.

Mumba P. (1995). *Child-to-Child and the growth chart: Its effects and influence on the girl child education.* Unpublished manuscript.

Mumba, P. (2000, July). *Democratisation of primary classrooms in Zambia: A case study of its implementation in a rural primary school in Mpika.* Paper presented at International Special Education Congress 2000, University of Manchester, UK. Retrieved from http://www.isec2000.org.uk/abstracts/papers_m/mumba_2.htm.

Mwape, G., & Serpell, R. (1996, August). Participatory appropriation of health science and technology. Poster presented at the International Conference of the International Society for the Study of Behavioural Development (ISSBD), Quebec, Canada. Retrieved from the ERIC database (ED417191).

Nsamenang, A. B. (1992). *Human development in cultural context: A third world perspective.* Newbury Park, CA: Sage.

Ogunnaike, O. A., & Houser, R. F. (2002). Yoruba toddlers' engagement in errands and cognitive performance on the Yoruba Mental Subscale. *International Journal of Behavioral Development, 26,*145–153.

Pridmore, P. (1999). *Participatory approaches to promoting health in schools: A Child to Child training manual.* London, UK: Institute of Education/CTC.

Rogoff, B. (1993). Observing sociocultural activity on three planes. In J. V. Wertsch, P. del Río, & A. Alvarez (Eds.), *Sociocultural studies of mind* (pp. 139–163). New York, NY: Cambridge University Press.

Salomon, G. (Ed.). (1993). *Distributed cognitions: Psychological and educational considerations.* Cambridge, England: Cambridge University Press.

Sameroff, A. J., & Fiese, B. H. (1992). Family representations of development. In I. E. Sigel, A. V. McGillicuddy-DeLisi, & J. J. Goodnow (Eds.), *Parental belief systems: The psychological consequences for children* (2nd ed., pp. 347–369). Hillsdale, NJ: Erlbaum.

Serpell, R. (1993a). *The significance of schooling: Life-journeys in an African society.* Cambridge, England: Cambridge University Press.

Serpell, R. (1993b). Interface between socio-cultural and psychological aspects of cognition: a commentary. In E. Forman, N. Minick, & A. Stone (Eds), *Contexts for learning: sociocultural dynamics* (pp.357–368). Oxford: Oxford University Press.

Serpell, R. (1996). Cultural models in indigenous socialization, and formal schooling in Zambia. In C.-P. Hwang, M. E. Lamb, & I. Sigel (Eds.), *Images of childhood* (pp. 129–142). Hillsdale, NJ: Erlbaum.

Serpell, R. (1999a). Theoretical conceptions of human development. In L. Eldering & P. Leseman (Eds.), *Effective early intervention: Cross-cultural perspectives* (pp. 41–66). New York, NY: Falmer.

Serpell, R. (1999b). Local accountability to rural communities: A challenge for educational planning in Africa. In F. Leach & A. Little (Eds.), *Education, cultures and economics: Dilemmas for development* (pp.107–135). New York, NY: Garland.

Serpell, R. (2001). Cultural dimensions of literacy promotion and schooling. In L. Verhoeven & C. Snow (Eds.), *Literacy and motivation* (pp. 243–273). Mahwah, NJ: Erlbaum.

Serpell, R. (2008). Participatory appropriation and the cultivation of nurturance: A case study of African primary health science curriculum development. In P. R. Dasen & A. Akkari (Eds.), *Educational theories and practices from the "majority world"* (pp. 71–97). New Delhi, India: Sage.

Serpell, R., & Chansa-Kabali, T. (2010, July). Developmental outcomes of enrolment in a Child-to-Child curriculum at a Zambian government primary school, 1995–2010. Paper presented at the 21st Biennial International Congress of the ISSBD, Lusaka, Zambia.

Serpell, R., & Hatano, G. (1997). Education, literacy and schooling. In J. W. Berry, R. Dasen, & T. S. Saraswathi (Eds.), *Handbook of cross-cultural psychology, Volume 2* (2nd ed., pp. 345–382). Boston, MA: Allyn & Bacon.

Serpell, R., & Mwape, G. (1998/99). Participatory appropriation of health science and technology: A case study of innovation in basic education in a rural district of Zambia. *African Social Research, 41/42,* 60–89.

Tharp, R. G., & Gallimore, R. (1988). *Rousing minds to life.* Cambridge, England: Cambridge University Press.

Udell, C. (2001). Educational innovation: A case study of Child-to-Child in Zambia (Unpublished master's thesis). University of Maryland, Baltimore County.

Valsiner, J. (1991). Social co-construction of psychological development from a comparative-cultural perspective. In J. Valsiner (Ed.), *Child development within culturally structured environments, Volume 3.* Norwood, NJ: Ablex.

Vygotsky, L. S. (1978). *Mind in society: The development of higher psychological processes.* (M. Cole, V. John-Steiner, S. Scribner, & E. Souberman, Eds.). Cambridge, MA: Harvard University Press.

Note

1. When quoting from the interviews in the main body of the text, we have cited only the serial number assigned to each respondent. The following code summarizes key demographic characteristics. F = female; M = male; T = completed some tertiary education; S = completed twelfth grade; B = completed ninth grade; P = stopped schooling after seventh grade; U = currently residing in an urban area; R = residing in a rural area; E = in formal employment; X = not in formal employment; S = full-time student; B = self-employed in business. For respondents quoted in this chapter, the details are as follows: 2: FTRX, 3: FTRE, 6: FTRE, 9: FTUE, 10: FTUX, 23: MTRE, 24: MTUE, 27: MBUX, 44BM: MTUE, 69: FTRE.

ROBERT SERPELL is professor of applied developmental psychology at the University of Zambia. E-mail: robertnserpell@gmail.com

PAUL MUMBA is a basic school teacher employed by the government of the Republic of Zambia. E-mail: chitimumba@yahoo.co.uk

TAMARA CHANSA-KABALI is lecturer in the psychology department at the University of Zambia. E-mail: tamarachansa@yahoo.com

NEW DIRECTIONS FOR CHILD AND ADOLESCENT DEVELOPMENT • DOI: 10.1002/cd

Flanagan, C. A., Martinez, M. L., Cumsille, P., & Ngomane, T. (2011). Youth civic development: Theorizing a domain with evidence from different cultural contexts. In C. A. Flanagan & B. D. Christens (Eds.), Youth civic development: Work at the cutting edge. New Directions for Child and Adolescent Development, 134, 95–109.

7

Youth Civic Development: Theorizing a Domain With Evidence From Different Cultural Contexts

Constance A. Flanagan, M. Loreto Martínez, Patricio Cumsille, Tsakani Ngomane

Abstract

The authors use examples of youth civic engagement from Chile, South Africa, Central/Eastern Europe, and the United States—and also emphasize diversities among youth from different subgroups within countries—to illustrate common elements of the civic domain of youth development. These include the primacy of collective activity for forming political identities and ideas and the greater heterogeneity of civic compared to other discretionary activities, the groupways or accumulated opportunities for acting due to the groups (social class, gender, ethnic, caste, etc.) to which a young person belongs, and the role of mediating institutions (schools, community-based organizations, etc.) as spaces where youths' actions contribute to political stability and change. © 2011 Wiley Periodicals, Inc.

Support for writing this chapter was provided by FONDECYT grant #1085231 awarded to M. Loreto Martínez. We also gratefully acknowledge support provided by a Resident Fellowship from the Spencer Foundation, by a Fulbright fellowship, and the Escuela de Psicología at the Pontificia Universidad Católica de Chile awarded to Constance Flanagan.

Over the past two decades the field of youth civic development has grown—in theoretical, empirical, and practical work. However, the extant body of scholarship has largely focused on youth in Western Europe and the United States. In this chapter, we extend this work with examples from Chile, South Africa, Central/Eastern Europe, and the Middle East to illustrate what we argue are common elements of the civic domain of youth development.

First, we emphasize the collective nature of the civic domain and the primacy of collaborative practice in the formation of adolescents' political views and identities. Second, we offer the concept of "groupways," an adaptation from cultural psychology's "selfways" (Markus, Mullally, & Kitayama, 1997), as a framework for theorizing about civic development. Although our concept applies to all groups, we focus on those at the periphery (i.e., ethnic or linguistic minorities, youth living in economically disadvantaged communities, sexual minority youth, etc.) rather than in the mainstream of their society to illustrate what we mean by the concept of groupways. Third, we discuss the role of mediating institutions in civil society—as spaces where adolescents act, and consequently where their political theories and identities are formed. Youths' actions in mediating institutions contribute both to political stability and to political change. Finally, we point to the role of younger generations in contributing to social change and of mediating institutions as spaces where they engage in social change.

The Primacy of Collaborative Practice

Vygotsky (1978) maintained that all ideas and beliefs are internalizations of social, collaborative practice. This premise is a fundamental starting point for the civic domain: to understand youth political development we must begin not with individual adolescents, but with the actions between individuals or in groups as our unit of analysis. For example, children's and adolescents' concepts of authority and beliefs about a person's right to share in decision making (a basic concept underlying sovereignty of the people) take shape in interactions with elders, parents, and teachers and in joint decision making with peers. Likewise, according to interviews with members of the Black Consciousness generation (born before 1963) in South Africa, their formation as political activists occurred in childhood as they witnessed the toll that grinding poverty and oppression took on their parents (Ngomane & Flanagan, 2003). Our main point is that the field of youth civic engagement needs to grapple with social interaction and collective action and the beliefs and attitudes that flow from them—a position that we emphasize because of the more typical focus in psychology on individual experience and development. In positing the primacy of joint action, we contend: (a) that civic/political goals are not accomplished by individuals acting alone, but rather by collective action; (b) that

NEW DIRECTIONS FOR CHILD AND ADOLESCENT DEVELOPMENT • DOI: 10.1002/cd

collective action does not imply the absence of diverse perspectives; and (c) that similar civic skills, identities, and dispositions are likely to develop via different relationships in various cultures.

To illustrate our first point, that civic goals are not accomplished by individuals acting alone, we draw from research on collective action to address the victimization of sexual minority youth in U.S. public schools. Sexual minority youth experience high levels of harassment in high schools that have enduring impacts on their mental health in young adulthood (Toomey, Ryan, Diaz, Card, & Russell, 2010). All too often, such harassment is either ignored or is dealt with as an individual or interpersonal problem. Contrast this way of addressing intolerance with the collective action of Gay-Straight Alliances (GSAs), student-led school-based groups that stand up against harassment and insist on tolerance and inclusion for all students in public schools. Not only does the presence of a GSA in their high-school increase the sense of safety and well-being of sexual minority youth (Goodenow, Szalacha, & Westheimer, 2006), but the collective identities formed in such groups empower participants (Russell, Muraco, Subramaniam, & Laub, 2009) and enable youth to challenge stigma (Meyer, 2003). In short, the collective action of a GSA has psychological benefits for participants and also achieves a political goal by changing the context for future cohorts of students.

Even in the face of very challenging situations, youth activist groups provide psychological benefits to members and nurture their civic dispositions. According to research with young Chilean activists, factors that contribute to their long-term commitment to political issues include the affective climate, interpersonal connections, opportunities for decision making in the organization, and the sense that their actions are both contributing to the goals of the organization and to society more broadly (Martínez, Peñaloza, & Valenzuela, 2011).

Concerning our second point, that collective action does not imply homogeneous perspectives, we maintain that grappling with diverse perspectives on issues may be a feature that distinguishes the benefits youth gain from action in the civic domain when compared to other forms of discretionary time use. Insofar as discretionary time use is voluntary, young people will typically be choosing activities they like. Consequently, they will be spending time in somewhat homogeneous groups—with others who have similar interests or who come from similar backgrounds. By contrast, in civic activities, youth are more likely to have heterogeneous encounters as they engage with individuals and groups whose experiences differ from their own. For example, in community volunteer work many young people gain a larger perspective about the lives of fellow members of their society (e.g., elderly, homeless, disabled)—groups of people they would seldom encounter in their everyday lives—and begin to see political issues from the points of view of those others (Flanagan, Gill, & Gallay, 2005).

NEW DIRECTIONS FOR CHILD AND ADOLESCENT DEVELOPMENT • DOI: 10.1002/cd

Similarly, in political activism the very act of taking a stand on an issue implies that youth confront points of view and political positions that differ from their own. According to research on youth activism, participation in activist projects shapes young people's intergroup understanding (Watkins, Larson, & Sullivan, 2007) as well as their strategic thinking abilities (Larson & Hansen, 2005). That said, simple exposure to diverse groups and perspectives is not enough for civic skill development or for intergroup understanding. According to research on intergroup dialogues, people (young and old alike) need to learn how to dialogue in ways that enable them to grapple with critical differences to move beyond group stereotypes toward intergroup understanding (Sorensen, Nagda, Gurin, & Maxwell, 2009).

As an example of our third point, that similar civic skills may develop through different cultural practices, we refer to the chapter by Serpell, Mumba, and Chansa-Kabali in this volume. They describe how children in the Child-to-Child program in Zambia were encouraged to air differences of opinion among peers (and in the process both males and females found their voices). However, in contrast to the Western tradition in which children sometimes gain their voices by disagreeing with parents and teachers, in Zambia the strong cultural traditions of respect for elders meant that children would not be encouraged to find their voices by challenging their elders, at least in public.

Groupways

Cultural psychologists coined the term *selfways* to refer to the accumulation of relationships and ways that an individual acts in the world that form the bases for his or her identity. In light of our emphasis on collective action as foundational for the civic domain, we have coined the term *groupways* to refer to the accumulation of activities and choices made over time by members of groups, choices shaped in fundamental ways by the position of status and power of their group in the larger polity. Young people's actions, choices, and the very possibilities they imagine are, borrowing from Erikson (1968), based on "ideological alternatives vitally related to the existing range of alternatives for identity formation" (p. 190). We submit that the *existing range* of alternatives that youth will imagine varies based on the social class, caste, racial/ethnic, religious, and gender groups to which they belong (e.g., indigenous Mapuche in Chile, Black South African students in Soweto, gay members of a U.S. high-school's gay-straight alliance). Research on adolescents' ethnic identity formation shows that young people consider certain options for identity meaningful because that is what their communities consider important (Phinney & Baldelomar, 2011). To this point our concept of groupways adds that meaningful identity options are constrained by what members of a group consider possible for people "like them."

Youths' awareness of their identities as members of particular groups develops, in part, from insights into how society treats people "like them" (i.e., as a member of a group at the periphery), and from the strengths they gain from organizing as part of a marginalized group. Concerning the latter, the chapter by Seif in this volume is illustrative. In the United States, Latina/os organizing for the Development, Relief and Education for Alien Minors (DREAM) Act and against exclusionary referenda in California united documented and undocumented immigrants in a common cause and identity. Even group stereotypes can be a means through which youth develop a collective, sometimes political consciousness. For example, Arab-American adolescents, who were cognizant of media images of their ethnic group as an "enemy" of America well before the terrorist attacks of September 11, 2001, were less likely than their co-ethnic peers (who were not as sensitive to this image) to believe that the government in the United States was responsive to all people and were more likely to interpret personal experiences of prejudice as acts of intolerance against their ethnic group (Wray-Lake, Syvertsen, & Flanagan, 2008).

Racial socialization research illustrates our concept of groupways and alludes to the possibility that ethnic minority children may learn political lessons about the position of their group in the larger polity. In raising their children, African American parents report that they sometimes warn their children about discrimination in society, prejudices that may pose barriers to the child's success (Hughes et al., 2006). These conversations often are prompted by an incident such as an exclusionary act toward the child from someone in authority or by an incident of discrimination that the parent experienced at work (Hughes & Chen, 1999). Thus, in preparing children to succeed, ethnic minority parents also are communicating information about how society sometimes treats people "like us." There are insidious and pervasive effects of racism and inequality on the everyday environments of ethnic minority children. Thus, whether or not it is articulated as "political" awareness, it may be more incumbent on ethnic minority children to understand the distinction between the public world "out there" and the private world inside our family—and how the one affects the other (Raffaelli, Carlo, Carranza, & Gonzales-Kruger, 2005). Because of the pervasive influence of racial discrimination in the United States, children in ethnic minority families may develop political insights, that is, awareness that the terms of the (equal opportunity) social contract in their polity do not apply equally to all groups.

Other research that illustrates our concept of groupways has shown that youths' perceptions of macro-level political and economic changes in their society reflect their awareness of the status of their group and of the implications of such changes for their group. Specifically, after the break-up of the Soviet Union in 1989, perceptions of the social and political changes taking place in their country among adolescents in Bulgaria, the Czech Republic, Hungary, and Russia differed based on whether the youth attended vocational or college-preparatory (gymnasium) schools. The former group, with fewer personal safety nets and who thus stood to "lose" under the terms of the new private market system to which their country was transitioning, were more likely to endorse the government's role in providing services and safety nets for citizens. They also were less likely than their peers in the college-preparatory schools to endorse school practices that increased students' autonomy and rights to disagree with teachers, practices that were synchronous with the characteristics of personality (individualism, self-determination, and self-sufficiency) expected in the new social order (Flanagan et al., 2003). Similarly, in the days when South Africa was going through its transformation to democracy, adolescents from different ethnic groups held different sociopolitical orientations reflective of the implications of the political changes for their group (Finchilescu & Dawes, 1998).

The accumulation of experiences implied in the construct means that groupways are not static; consequently, neither are youths' political views. A good example comes from Black South Africans, who, as adolescents, were isolated in their rural communities under apartheid. The opportunity in the 1980s to attend agricultural colleges away from their village opened their minds and they began to imagine alternative future scenarios for their country, futures that they had not envisioned before they left home (Ngomane & Flanagan, 2003). Black South African youth from different ethnic groups got to know one another in these settings and, consistent with our earlier emphasis on the importance of collaborative practice, together they dreamed and discussed alternatives to the apartheid system and choices they could make to realize those visions. As the slogan of the World Social Forum suggests, they began to believe that "another world was possible" (see Fisher & Ponniah, 2003).

As noted, the political choices of young people are shaped by the range of alternatives they imagine are possible and that range of options will vary at different historical moments. Because the adolescent and young adult years are a time when political identities and views crystallize, the historical era when a generation of youth comes of age is likely to be formative of that generation's political views and behaviors into adulthood. For example, among young adults in the United States, levels of social trust (beliefs that people generally are trustworthy) tend to increase toward the end of the third decade of life as individuals settle into social roles and as their lives become less episodic, more predictable. However, that increase is relative to each cohort's initial level of social trust in late adolescence; so, if a cohort begins at lower levels of social trust in late adolescence, his or her trust in others will increase as the cohort matures, but his or her endpoint at age thirty will not reach the levels of other cohorts who came of age at a more "trusting" time (Briddell et al., 2009).

Another example of the significance of the historical era when youth come of age is based on comparing the forms of civic action chosen by (or available to) different generations of Black South African activists. The postdemocracy generation came of age after apartheid had been dismantled. Thus, the political movement that had burnished their parents' and grandparents' activism was no longer a cause that they could join. For the postdemocracy generation of Black South Africans there were more choices for individuals but also less urgency and clarity about political activism. Perhaps it is not surprising then, that compared to those cohorts who came of age during the apartheid era, the postdemocracy generation was less politically active and less militant. Fewer defined themselves as activists, and those who did found outlets mainly in local indigenous, religious, and community-based grassroots groups (Ngomane, 2005).

Finally, groupways refers not only to the way members of groups act in the world, but also to the meaning associated with their actions. Similar political actions may have very different implications for youth development, depending, in part, on the meaning of the youths' cause in their community. This point is clearly demonstrated in Barber's (2008) comparisons of political activism among Bosnian versus Palestinian youth. Although ethnicity figured in each group's actions, Palestinian youth understood their activism as part of the larger struggle of their people. Bosnian youth had no intergenerational struggle as a context; instead, they learned about and had to defend their Muslim identities through sudden attacks from Serbian (former) neighbors and friends. Hence, the collective identity that empowered Palestinian youth was experienced by Bosnians from a standpoint of victimization.

Civil Society: Mediating Institutions

Adolescents' experiences of the public (government) and private (economic) sectors of society are indirect for the most part. Some may work for a wage; few are eligible to vote. Yet, in the course of growing up, most will come to adopt the political and economic principles that govern everyday life in their society. We contend that this is due to their actions and experiences in mediating institutions—schools, ethnic/community, cultural, and faith-based groups (see also, Flanagan, Martinez, & Cumsille, 2011). In choosing the term, mediating institutions, we emphasize that these settings function as *interpretive* spaces. The practices of these settings are shaped by the policies and mores of the dominant social order. At the same time, mediating institutions also can be settings where people gather and challenge their government to take actions to protect citizens. We are not arguing, as others have (see Berger, Neuhaus, & Novak, 1996), that so-called mediating structures are a substitute for public services and programs, but rather that they are spaces where citizens' actions both shape and are shaped by the political order. Mediating institutions play a formative role insofar as citizens themselves are shaped by their actions in these settings. For example, schools and community-based institutions serve as "mini polities" where younger generations can explore what it means to be a member of a political community and can practice the rights and obligations associated with membership in that community (Flanagan, Stoppa, Syvertsen, & Stout, 2010).

Social Stability. Mediating institutions are spaces where the political and economic principles of a society are interpreted—reinforced, challenged, and renegotiated. Activities in these settings contribute both to political stability and to political change. Concerning the former, we draw from the notion of practices in cultural psychology. Practices are routine ways of acting that are followed by most of the people in one's group. Because they are both routine and because everyone "like me" does them, these practices tend to reinforce beliefs that they are the natural, proper, perhaps the *only* way to do things (Goodnow, 2011).

For example, in most societies, schools encourage students' identification with the dominant culture through three common sets of practices: through the ethnocentric biases of curricula, through explicit positive narratives about the nation's history, and through adoption of symbols and practices of civil culture (Barrett, 2007). Consequently, dominant cultural views gain hegemony and often are adopted even by groups whose interests are marginalized by those views (Gramsci, 1971). Ultimately, in the absence of competing narratives, many members of a younger generation will adopt as natural and proper the mores, values, and principles that make their social order work.

At a macro level, the process of political stability depends on societies being not just economic and political systems with constitutions, laws, and institutions, but also thinking systems with beliefs and practices widely endorsed by the society's members. Such thinking systems are produced because culture and cognition are mutually constitutive (Cole, 1996; see also edited volume by Jensen, 2011) and because cultural ideals and values guide people's normative beliefs and goals, including their beliefs and goals for children's development (Rogoff, 2003). Changing these beliefs and values, these "thinking systems," is an uphill battle. According to system justification theory, conservatism (defending the status quo) enjoys a psychological advantage over challenges to the way things are because people tend to dismiss the possibility of change and because conservative ideologies are generally simpler, more internally consistent, and less subject to ambiguity compared to liberal ones (Jost, Banaji, & Nosek, 2004). Ironically, critiquing the system may be easier for the privileged than for the disadvantaged because of the safety nets associated with privilege and the absence of alternatives for the disadvantaged. For example, adolescents from poor communities in the United States who remain in school, despite high dropout rates in their school districts, are more likely than their peers in wealthier school districts to hold individuals accountable for being poor or unemployed and are less likely to blame the system (Flanagan & Tucker, 1999). As system justification theory argues, legitimizing the system restores a sense of confidence and control, especially for those who are confronted by and do not have other ways to manage uncertainty (Jost et al., 2004).

Routine practices in mediating institutions that look the same on the surface may convey different political messages depending on how the practices are combined (Vygotsky, 1978). For example, in one comparative study across six nations, it was common practice for children to do household chores and it was also common for parents to give their children some form of allowance or pocket money. Only in some nations were these two practices linked and the rationale for why children should do chores varied as well—according to the dominant principles of economic organization in those societies. Youth from nations with a strong social welfare contract felt that doing chores taught children responsibility for the group (i.e., social responsibility), whereas responsibility for oneself was the rationale in those nations with more liberal economies. Further, in the latter (liberal economy) nations, adolescents were more likely to say that children should earn allowances for doing chores, suggesting that they had adopted notions of wage work that were dominant in their societies (Bowes, Flanagan, & Taylor, 2001). (See also the discussion by Serpell et al. in this volume on how the Chewa in Eastern Zambia conceive of an intelligent person not simply as one who has gone to school, but as one who applies his or her learning in a socially responsible way.)

Social Change. Besides their role in stabilizing polities, mediating institutions also provide the "free spaces" where youth can challenge the status quo, participate in governance, and gain democratic skills. In the process, they also can build the foundations for social change. Evans and Boyte (1992), who coined the term *free spaces* explain the concept by referring to the collective actions of Black slaves in the United States who transformed the very Christian religion that was supposed to convince them to accept their oppression—into symbols and aspirations for a better (and freer) life for their people. Similarly, as we already noted, agricultural colleges functioned as a free space for Black South African students to imagine together an alternative to apartheid society. In short, mediating institutions can serve as free spaces where, collectively, people imagine alternatives to the way things are and by acting together, develop the skills to realize that vision.

Concerning social change, we emphasize three points about activities in mediating institutions. First, it is tempting to conceive of social change as if it occurs suddenly—at particular historical moments (consider the episodic way in which the media portrayed the popular uprisings of 2011 in several nations of the Middle East or the fall of the Berlin Wall in 1989 or the framing of the Civil Rights Movement in U.S. textbooks as the result of one woman's refusal to sit in the back of the bus). However, it is a coalescence of forces built over time that makes these events happen. In the free spaces of civil society (what we are calling mediating institutions), criticism of the status quo and actions that challenge it provide the foundations for social change. For example, among the factors that contributed to the break-up of the Soviet Union were environmental movements in Central and Eastern Europe that challenged the state's negligence, second economy experiments of families starting small businesses, and the fascination with the West in youth culture. Similarly, in Chile, university students' associations in the 1960s led a national movement of changing the university from an Ivory Tower removed from society to one with responsibilities to society. Students' movements also were instrumental with labor and other sectors in electing a socialist government in 1970. A decade later Chilean youth had a leading role in the resistance mobilization (e.g., street protests) against the military regime during the late 1980s that ultimately led to its demise (Martínez & Cumsille, 2011).

The Arab spring of 2011 also was not, as the media made it seem, either leaderless or spontaneous. In fact, despite decades of authoritarian rule that crushed the formation of civil society organizations and of alternative political parties, the April 6th Youth Movement was the culmination of several years' work in which youth groups who had been meeting in smaller cells, and using the latest in information technology, learned the strategies, tactics, and discipline of organizers in other countries (Al Jazeera English, 2011). Demographic factors also made the conditions ripe for a popular uprising. Over the past four decades, there have been exponential improvements in health, life expectancy, and the percentage of children in education, which led to higher expectations among the people for self-rule. The youth bulge, especially the growth in university-educated middle-class youth with few life prospects, was critical to the crystallization of a collective challenge to autocratic rule (Kimenyi, 2011).

Second, activities in mediating institutions also contribute to social change because young people engage in multiple settings where different routines are practiced and different values reinforced. For example, hegemonic values and beliefs may be learned in school, but challenged at home. This was precisely the case in Chile in the years leading up to the 1990 popular elections that voted Pinochet out of power. For more than a decade of the military rule, routine practices in schools reinforced positive affection for the regime. On a daily basis, school children pledged allegiance and were surrounded by national symbols of unity. Yet they heard competing political messages in other mediating institutions, such as the safe spaces of their families.

Social change also occurs because the *rules* are constantly being negotiated by various actors within particular settings. One of the best examples is the intergenerational dynamics in the families of new immigrants—as parents and children negotiate within-family relationships and redefine their group's identity in the new society that they have entered. These experiences inform different sets of ideas—that move back and forth between mediating institutions—and ultimately fuel social change (see also Seif, this volume). In some cases, it is the younger generation in new immigrant communities who are taking collective action as spokespeople for their families and communities (Christens & Dolan, 2011).

Finally, despite the case we made above for the hegemony and repeated enactments of cultural practices, some youth may challenge the dominant narratives and practices of mainstream institutions. An iconic example is the revolt of elementary and secondary students in Soweto, South Africa, against the use of Afrikans as the official language in their instruction. Of course, that practice was symbolic of a larger political injustice—the separate and inferior quality of the education of Black children and the second-class status and outright abuse of their people under apartheid.

A similar student-led revolt occurred in Chile in 2006. The "Penguin Revolution" was a massive protest against the unequal and highly segregated (public and private) system of education—by students from across the educational tiers and representing different social strata. These students considered it unjust that some among them enjoyed the benefits of quality education while their peers did not. Both the Penguin and Soweto protests were led by adolescents and both motivated public discussions and moved other sectors of society (labor unions, churches, teachers, government officials, and legislators) to action.

In fact, compared to their lower levels of participation in electoral politics, youth tend to be disproportionately represented in movements for social change. As contemporary work with Chilean activists suggests, they are motivated to challenge and transform a social order that they consider unjust (Martínez, Silva, Carmona, & Cumsille, 2011). Their stance reflects their criticism of the liberal market economy that excludes and marginalizes the less privileged from exercising their social and political rights (Silva & Silva, 2010). Furthermore, even among youth who are less committed to activism, themes of socioeconomic disparities and the gulf between ordinary citizens and the political elite figure in young Chileans' conceptualization of citizenship (Martínez, Silva, & Hernández, 2010).

Youth engaged in projects for social change are addressing some social justice issues—inadequate housing, food insecurity, polluted lakes and rivers. When youth act on these issues, they internalize knowledge that is emotionally charged. As others have noted, compared to knowledge about the natural or physical world, knowledge about society is "hot" (Hatano & Takahashi, 2005; see also edited volume by Barrett & Buchanan-Barrow, 2005). Consequently, it may be more difficult to separate what we "know" about a civic issue from how we "feel" about it. In fact, passion about a social issue may motivate a search for knowledge about it. Ultimately, emotions impact our motivation to learn and our interpretation of *the facts* in the civic domain.

Younger Generations and Social Change

Historically, youth are more likely than their elders to participate in movements for social change. This may be due to their idealism, their willingness to take risks, or the fact that they have a greater stake than their elders in defining what the future might promise. Because of their position on the brink of adulthood, youth are pressed to explore future possibilities for their own lives; in so doing, they also will confront questions of where their world is headed. These are political questions because they concern the polis and the ties that bind people as citizens of local communities and global worlds.

Widespread cultural beliefs and routine practices tend to reinforce the status quo but younger generations never carbon copy the political world that is handed down to them. In fact, younger generations always contribute to social change, if for no other reason than the fact that they replace their elders as a share of society's membership and as a new generation, they view the issues of their society through a "fresh lens" (Mannheim, 1928/1952). They also are less committed to social roles that may constrain the futures they envision. As Erikson (1968) noted, youth take an active role in reinterpreting, in the context of the historical era when they come of age, various tenets of the dominant ideologies of their societies: "youth can offer its loyalties and energies both to the conservation of that which continues to feel true and to the correction of that which has lost its regenerative significance" (p. 134).

References

Al Jazeera English. (2011, February 9). People and power—Egypt: Seeds of change. Retrieved from www.youtube.com/watch?v=QrNz0dZgqN8.

Barber, B. K. (2008). Contrasting portraits of war: Youths' varied experiences with political violence in Bosnia and Palestine. *International Journal of Behavioral Development*, 32(4), 298–309.

Barrett, M. (2007). *Children's knowledge, beliefs, and feelings about nations and national groups.* East Sussex, UK: Psychology Press.

Barrett, M., & Buchanan-Barrow, E. (Eds.). (2005). *Children's understanding of society.* East Sussex, England: Psychology Press.

Berger, M. L., Neuhaus, R. J., & Novak, M. (1996). *To empower people: From state to Civil Society.* Washington, DC: American Enterprise Institute.

Bowes, J. M., Flanagan, C., & Taylor, A. J. (2001). Adolescents' ideas about individual and social responsibility in relation to children's household work: Some international comparisons. *International Journal of Behavioral Development*, 25, 60–68. doi:10.1080/01650250042000032

Briddell, L., Wray-Lake, L., Syvertsen, A. K., Flanagan, C. A., Osgood, D. W., Bachman, J. G., . . . Schulenberg, J. E. (2009, April). *Role transitions and social trust: A study of late adolescence.* Paper presented at the meetings of the Society for Research on Child Development, Denver, CO.

Christens, B. D., & Dolan, T. (2011). Interweaving youth development, community development, and social change through youth organizing. *Youth & Society*, 43(2), 528–548. doi:10.1177/0044118X10383647

Cole, M. (1996). *Cultural psychology: A once and future discipline.* Cambridge, MA: Harvard University Press.

Erikson, E. H. (1968). *Identity: Youth and crisis.* New York, NY: W.W. Norton.

Evans, S. M., & Boyte, H. C. (1992). *Free spaces: The sources of democratic change in America.* Chicago, IL: University of Chicago Press.

Finchilescu, G., & Dawes, A. (1998). Catapulted into democracy: South African adolescents' sociopolitical orientations following rapid social change. *Journal of Social Issues, 54*(3), 563–583. doi:10.1111/j.1540-4560.1998.tb01236.x

Fisher, W. F., & Ponniah, T. (Eds.) (2003). *Another world is possible: Popular alternatives to globalization at the World Social Forum.* London, England: Zed Books.

Flanagan, C. A., Campbell, B., Botcheva, L., Bowes, J., Csapo, B., Macek, P., & Sheblanova, E. (2003). Social class and adolescents' beliefs about justice in different social orders. *Journal of Social Issues, 59*(4), 711–732. doi:10.1046/j.0022-4537.2003 .00086.x

Flanagan, C. A., Gill, S., & Gallay, L. S. (2005). Social participation and social trust in adolescence: The importance of heterogeneous encounters. In A. Omoto (Ed.), *Processes of community change and social action* (pp. 149–166). Mahwah, NJ: Erlbaum.

Flanagan, C., Martinez, M. L., & Cumsille, P. (2011). Civil societies as developmental and cultural contexts for civic identity formation. In L. Arnett Jensen (Ed.), *Bridging cultural and developmental psychology: New syntheses in theory, research and policy* (pp. 113–137). New York, NY: Oxford University Press.

Flanagan, C., Stoppa, T., Syvertsen, A., & Stout, M. (2010). Schools and social trust. In L. Sherrod, J. Torney-Purta, & C. A. Flanagan (Eds.), *Handbook of research on civic engagement in youth* (pp. 307–329). Hoboken, NJ: Wiley.

Flanagan, C. A., & Tucker, C. J. (1999). Adolescents' explanations for political issues: Concordance with their views of self and society. *Developmental Psychology, 35*(5), 1198–1209. doi:10.1037/0012-1649.35.5.1198

Goodenow, C., Szalacha, L., & Westheimer, K. (2006). School support groups, other school factors, and the safety of sexual minority adolescents. *Psychology in the Schools, 43,* 573–589. doi:10.1002/pits.20173

Goodnow, J. J. (2011). Merging cultural and psychological accounts of family contexts. In L. Arnett Jensen (Ed.), *Bridging cultural and developmental psychology: New syntheses in theory, research and policy* (pp. 73–91). New York, NY: Oxford University Press.

Gramsci, A. (1971). *Selections from the prison notebooks.* New York, NY: International Press.

Hatano, G., & Takahashi, K. (2005). The development of societal cognition: A commentary. In M. Barrett & E. Buchanan-Barrow (Eds.), *Children's understanding of society* (pp. 287–303). East Sussex, England: Psychology Press.

Hughes, D., & Chen, L. (1999). The nature of parents' race-related communications to children: A developmental perspective. In L. Balater & C. S. Tamis-LeMonda (Eds.), *Child psychology: A handbook of contemporary issues* (pp. 467–490). Philadelphia, PA: Taylor and Francis Psychology Press.

Hughes, D., Rodriguez, J., Smith, E. P., Johnson, D. J., Stevenson, H. C., & Spicer, P. (2006). Parents' ethnic-racial socialization practices: A review of research and directions for future study. *Developmental Psychology, 42,* 747–770. doi:10.1037 /0012-1649.42.5.747

Jensen, L. A. (Ed.). (2011). *Bridging cultural and developmental psychology: New syntheses in theory, research and policy.* New York, NY: Oxford University Press.

Jost, J. T., Banaji, M. R., & Nosek, B. A. (2004). A decade of system justification theory: Accumulated evidence of conscious and unconscious bolstering of the status quo. *Political Psychology, 25,* 881–920. doi:10.1111/j.1467-9221.2004.00402.x

Kimenyi, M. S. (2011). The Arab democracy paradox. Washington, DC: The Brookings Institution. Retrieved from www.brookings.edu/opinions/2011/0304_arab _democracy_kimenyi.aspx.

Larson, R., & Hansen, D. (2005).The development of strategic thinking: Learning to impact human systems in a youth activism program. *Human Development, 48,* 327-349.

Mannheim, K. (1952). The problem of generations. In P. Kecshevich (Ed.), *Essays on the sociology of knowledge* (pp. 276–322). London, England: Routledge & Kegan Paul. (Original work published 1928)

Markus, H. R., Mullally, P., & Kitayama, S. (1997). Selfways: Diversity in modes of cultural participation. In U. Neisser & D. Jopling (Eds.), *The conceptual self in context: Culture, experience, self-understanding* (pp. 13–61). Cambridge, England: Cambridge University Press.

Martínez, M. L., & Cumsille, P. (2011). Chile. In J. J. Arnett (Ed.), *Adolescent psychology around the world.* New York, NY: Psychology Press.

Martínez, M. L., Peñaloza, P., & Valenzuela, C. (2011). *Civic commitment in young activists: Emergent processes in the development of their personal and collective identity.* Submitted for publication.

Martínez, M. L., Silva, C., Carmona, M., & Cumsille, P. (2011). *Young Chileans' views of citizenship: Findings from the first generation born after the reinstitution of democracy.* Submitted for publication.

Martínez, M. L., Silva, C., & Hernández, A. C. (2010). ¿En qué ciudadanía creen los jóvenes? Creencias, aspiraciones de ciudadanía y motivaciones para la participación sociopolítica [What type of citizenship do youth believe in? Beliefs, aspirations, and motivations for sociopolitical participation]. *Psykhe, 2(2),* 25–37. doi:10.4067/S0718-22282010000200004

Meyer, I. H. (2003). Prejudice, social stress, and mental health in lesbian, gay, and bisexual populations: Conceptual issues and research evidence. *Psychological Bulletin, 129,* 674–697. doi:10.1037/0033-2909.129.5.674

Ngomane, T. (2005). *Civic participation: The emergence of political leadership in South Africa* (Unpublished doctoral dissertation). The Pennsylvania State University, University Park.

Ngomane, T., & Flanagan, C. (2003). The road to democracy in South Africa. *Peace Review, 15(3),* 267–271. doi:10.1080/1040265032000130841

Phinney, J. S., & Baldelomar, O. A. (2011). Identity development in multiple cultural contexts. In L. A. Jensen (Ed.), *Bridging cultural and developmental approaches to psychology* (pp. 161–186). New York, NY: Oxford University Press.

Raffaelli, M., Carlo, G., Carranza, M. A., & Gonzales-Kruger, G. E. (2005). Understanding Latino children and adolescents in the mainstream: Placing culture in the center of developmental models. In L. A. Jensen & R. W. Larson (Eds.), *New horizons in developmental theory and research* (pp. 23–32). San Francisco, CA: Jossey-Bass.

Rogoff, B. (2003). *The cultural nature of human development.* New York, NY: Oxford University Press.

Russell, S. T., Muraco, A., Subramaniam, A., & Laub, C. (2009). Youth empowerment and high school Gay-Straight Alliances. *Journal of Youth and Adolescence. 38,* 891–903.

Seif, H. (2011). "Unapologetic and unafraid": Immigrant youth come out from the shadows. In C. A. Flanagan & B. D. Christens (Eds.), Youth civic development: Work at the cutting edge. *New Directions for Child and Adolescent Development, 134,* 59–75.

Serpell, R., Mumba, P., & Chansa-Kabali, T. (2011). Early educational foundations for the development of civic responsibility: An African experience. In C. A. Flanagan & B. D. Christens (Eds.), Youth civic development: Work at the cutting edge. *New Directions for Child and Adolescent Development, 134,* 77–93.

Silva, E., & Silva, C. (2010). La economía política y las motivaciones de participación socio-política de Jóvenes Chilenos: Una interpretación de los Hallazgos de Martínez,

Silva y Hernández [Political economy and motivations for sociopolitical participation in Chilean youth: An interpretation of the findings of Martínez, Silva and Hernández]. *Psykhe, 19*(2), 39–50. doi:10.4067/S0718-22282010000200005

Sorensen, N., Nagda, B. A., Gurin, P., & Maxwell, K. E. (2009). Taking a "hands on" approach to diversity in higher education: A critical-dialogic model for effective intergroup interaction. *Analyses of Social Issues and Public Policy, 9*(1), 3–35. doi:10.1111/j.1530-2415.2009.01193.x

Toomey, R. B., Ryan, C., Diaz, R., Card, N. A., & Russell, S. T. (2010). Gender nonconforming lesbian, gay, bisexual, and transgender youth: School victimization and young adult psychosocial adjustment. *Developmental Psychology, 46*, 1580–1589. doi:10.1037/a0020705

Vygotsky, L. S. (1978). *Mind in society: The development of higher psychological processes.* Cambridge, MA: Harvard University Press.

Watkins, N., Larson, R., & Sullivan, P. (2007). Learning to bridge difference: Community youth programs as contexts for developing multicultural competencies. *American Behavioral Scientist, 51*, 380–402.

Wray-Lake, L., Syvertsen, A. B., & Flanagan, C. (2008). Contested citizenship and social exclusion: Adolescent Arab-American immigrants' views of the "Social Contract." *Applied Developmental Science, 12*, 84–92. doi:10.1080/10888690801997085

CONSTANCE A. FLANAGAN is professor of human ecology at the University of Wisconsin–Madison. E-mail: caflanagan@wisc.edu

M. LORETO MARTÍNEZ is professor of psychology at Pontificia Universidad Católica de Chile. E-mail: mlmartig@uc.cl

PATRICIO CUMSILLE is professor of psychology at Pontificia Universidad Católica de Chile. E-mail: pcumsill@uc.cl

TSAKANI NGOMANE is program leader for extension services in the Department of Agricultural Economics, Extension and Rural Development at the University of Pretoria, South Africa. E-mail: Tsakani.Ngomane@up.ac.za

INDEX

Abdul-Adil, J., 49
Abrego, L., 68
Activism Orientation Scale (AOS), 51
Ahmed, N., 15
Alinsky, S. D., 38
Alisat, S., 13, 50
Allen, N. E., 37
Altman, I., 37
Amanti, C., 37
Arnold, M., 16, 19
Astuto, J., 15, 16
Atkins, R., 15, 20
Attribution theory, 52–54

Bach, R., 62
Bada, X., 60
Baldelomar, O. A., 98
Ballinger, J., 14
Banaji, M. R., 102
Bandura, A., 18
Barber, C., 63, 101
Barrett, M., 102, 105
Batalova, J., 70
Batson, C., 15
Baumeister, R. F., 13
Beebe, T., 20
Benson, P. L., 2
Berger, M. L., 101
Berkas, T. H., 20
Berman, S., 12, 14
Black Racial Identity Scale, 53
Bloemraad, I., 60
Blustein, D. L., 47, 48
Blyth, D. A., 20
Bohanek, J. G., 86
Bowes, J. M., 103
Boyd, D., 13, 16
Boyte, H. C., 103
Brennan, W., 63
Briddell, L., 17, 100
Brodkin, K., 64
Bronfenbrenner, U., 17, 36, 90
Buchanan-Barrow, E., 105
Burns, N., 18

Camino, L., 28, 34, 35
Cammarota, J., 31, 32
Campbell, C., 49

Campbell, D. E., 18
Candee, D., 12
Cao Yu, H., 34
Card, N. A., 97
Care and justice, 14
Carlo, G., 16, 99
Carlson, E. D., 48
Carmona, M., 105
Carranza, M. A., 99
Chamberlain, R. M., 48
Chansa-Kabali, T., 5, 7, 77, 78, 86, 93
Chavous, T. M., 53
Checkoway, B. N., 29
Chen, L., 99
Child-to-Child (CtC) curriculum, description of, 5, 7, 77, 78, 80–86, 98
Christens, B. D., 1, 4, 7, 9, 27, 29, 30, 32, 33, 34, 37, 38, 41, 105
CIRCLE (www.civicyouth.org), 2
Citizenship, three forms of, 44
Cognitive awakening, 49
Cognitive development, social responsibility and, 14, 15–16
Cognitive Empowerment Scale, 51
Cohn, D., 61
Cole, M., 90, 102
Coleman, M. N., 48
Coming Out of the Shadows Week, 71
Contra Costa Interfaith Supporting Community Organization (CCISCO), 30
Cooke, D. Y., 53
Cooperative learning, 83–84
Corning, A. F., 51
Coronado, H., 65, 66
Correa, C., 88
Cortés, R., 65, 66
Costanza-Chock, S., 71
Côté, J. E., 16
Critical action, 46–47, 50–51
Critical consciousness: components of, 46–51; defined, 4, 46; empowerment theory and, 51, 53; future directions for research on, 52–53
Critical reflection, 46, 47–50, 52
Cumsille, P., 5, 7, 13, 95, 101, 104, 105, 109

D'Andrade, R., 90
Dasen, P. R., 80
Dawes, A., 100
Delgado, M., 29, 34
Diaz, R., 97
Diemer, M. A., 4, 7, 32, 43, 46, 47, 48, 57
Doe, Plyer v., 63
Dolan, T., 33, 34, 35, 37, 38, 105
Donnelly, T M., 20
DREAM (Development, Relief, and Education for Alien Minors) Act, 60, 62, 63, 67, 69–73, 99
DREAMers, 68, 69–70

Eisenberg, N., 15, 16, 18, 19
Empowerment theory, 51, 53
Engbretson, J., 48
Enyedy, N., 33
Erikson, E. H., 17, 98, 106
Errands, sending children on, 80
Espinoza, R., 65, 66
Evans, S. M., 103

Falconer, J. W., 48
Fanon, F., 45
Fegley, S., 15, 16, 17
Fiese, B. H., 90
Finchilescu, G., 100
Fisher, R., 29
Fisher, W. F., 100
Fivush, R., 86
Flanagan, C. A., 1, 2, 5, 7, 9, 13, 17, 19, 46, 53, 95, 96, 97, 99, 100, 101, 102, 103, 109
Fletcher, A., 34
Flores-Gonzáles, N., 60, 62
Fox, J., 60
Free spaces, defined, 103
Freire, P., 4, 31, 32, 43, 44, 45, 46, 47, 52–55
Friendships, as gateways to social responsibility, 19–20
Furco, A., 2
Furnham, A., 13

Gallay, L., 12, 13, 97
Gallimore, R., 83
Gandhi, M., 52
Gay-Straight Alliances (GSAs), 97
Geil, K., 33, 37
Gender equality, Child-to-Child curriculum and, 88
Gill, S., 13, 97

Gilligan, C., 14
Ginwright, S., 33, 34, 53
Gonzalez, N., 37
Gonzales, R. G., 66, 68, 69
Gonzales-Kruger, G. E., 99
Goodenow, C., 97
Goodnow, J. J., 18, 19, 102
Gramsci, A., 102
Griffith, D. M., 49
Grigorenko, E. L., 80
Group discussion, 54
Groupways, description of, 6, 96, 98–101
Grusec, J. E., 18, 19
Guessous, O., 49
Gurin, P., 98
Gutierrez, L., 29, 34

Hacker, J. S., 29
Hamilton, S. F., 2
Hamme, C. L., 51
Hanft, S., 34, 35
Hansen, K., 78, 98
Hart, D., 15, 16, 17, 20
Hatano, G., 79, 105
Hattam, V., 71
Hawes, H., 82
Helwig, C. C., 16
Hernández, A. C., 105
Hitlin, S., 12, 16, 22
Hoffman, M. L., 15, 16, 19
Holland, R. W., 13
Holmes, D., 48
Hoppers, W., 88
Hosang, D. W., 28
Houser, R. F., 80
Hsieh, C., 46
Hughes, D., 99
Hugo Lopez, M., 61
Hunsberger, B., 13, 50

Identity development, 16–17
Immigrant student groups, 68–69
Inhibition, defined, 15
Interpretive spaces, 101

James, T., 53
Javdani, S., 38
Jennings, M. K., 21
Jensen, L. A., 102
Johnson, M. K., 20
Jones, H., 37
Jones, M., 71
Jost, J. T., 102, 103

Kahne, J., 14, 21, 44
Kauffman, A., 46
Kaunda, K., 5, 82
Kieffer, C. H., 50
Kielsmeier, J. C., 20
Kimenyi, M. S., 104
Kingsley, P. R., 80
Kirby, E. H., 61
Kirshner, B., 4, 7, 27, 33, 34, 37, 41
Kitayama, S., 16, 96
Knight, G. P., 16
Koenig, N., 46
Kohlberg, L., 12, 14
Kuczynski, L., 19

Labissiere, C. Y., 63
Lacoe, J., 34
Larson, R. W., 33, 98
Laser, J. A., 35
Latina/o youth: cultural values of, 64; demographic patterns of, 61–62; in immigration protests, 72; political consciousness of, 4–5
Latino organizing for DREAM Act, 5, 73, 99. See also DREAM (Development, Relief, and Education for Alien Minors) Act
Laub, C., 97
Leary, M. R., 13
Leibowitz, G. S., 35
Lerner, J. V., 13
Lerner, R. M., 13
Levine, B., 80
Levine, R., 80, 88
Levine, S., 88
Lewin, K., 7
Lewis-Charp, H., 34
Li, C., 13, 47
Lloyd, C. B., 2
Lopez, M. H., 61, 63

Madera, G., 69
Malle, B. F., 48
Mannheim, K., 106
Mapp, K. L., 37
Marcelo, K. B., 61, 63
Markus, H. R., 16, 96
Martín-Baró, I., 53, 54
Martínez, M. L., 5, 7, 95, 97, 101, 104, 105, 109
Marx, K., 45
Maxwell, K. E., 98
Mayton, D. M. II, 13
McHugh, M., 70

MacPhail, C., 49
Mediating institutions: defined, 101, 102; role of, 101–105
Mediratta, K., 34, 35
Memmi, A., 45
Mendoza, A. A., 67
Meyer, I. H., 97
Middaugh, E., 21
Mira, M., 29, 34
Moll, L. C., 37
Montero, M., 54
Morley, D., 81
Morrell, M. E., 33, 50
Morris, P. A., 17
Mortimer, J. T., 20
Mullally, P., 96
Mumba, P., 5, 7, 77, 78, 82, 83, 85, 86, 89, 93
Muraco, A., 97
Mussen, P., 16, 18
Mwape, G., 82
Myers, D. J., 51

Nagda, B. A., 98
Neff, D., 37
Neuhaus, R. J., 101
Neville, H. A., 48
Ngomane, T., 5, 7, 95, 96, 100, 101, 109
Nikundiwe, T., 29, 34
Nosek, B. A., 102
Novak, M., 101
Nsamenang, A. B., 80

Obama, B., 60, 70
Ogunnaike, O. A., 80
Opportunities to practice social responsibility, 19–21
Orellana, M. F., 64
Osgood, D. W., 17

Pancer, S. M., 13, 50
Participatory action research (PAR), 31, 33–34, 54, 55
Passel, J. S., 61
Peñaloza, P., 97
Penguin Revolution, 105
Perez, W., 65, 66
Pérez Huber, L., 68
Perla, H., 65
Peterson, C., 16
Peterson, N. A., 51
Peterson, T. H., 34, 35
Petrokubi, J., 34, 35
Phinney, J. S., 98

Pierson, P., 29
Piliavin, J. A., 22
Pillai, S., 28
Pinochet, A., 104
Plyler v. Doe, 63
Political efficacy, defined, 46, 50
Ponniah, T., 100
Portes, A., 62
Pozzoboni, K., 37
Pratt, M., 13, 19, 50
Pratto, F., 48
Pridmore, P., 82
Proposition 187, California voter initiative, 62
Prosocial behaviors, modeling, 18. *See also* Child-to-Child (CtC) curriculum; Social responsibility
Public relationships, defined, 32
Putnam, R. D., 2, 17

Raffaelli, M. 99
Ramos, K., 65, 66
Rappaport, J., 46
Reich, G., 67
Reynolds, J., 64
Richman, A., 88
Riecken, J., 49
Riecken, T., 49
Rincón, A., 67, 68, 69
Rogers, J., 34, 66
Rogoff, B., 37, 81, 102
Romero, A. F., 31
Root, S., 2
Ruck, M. D., 15, 16
Russell, S. T., 33, 97
Ryan, C., 97

Sadovsky, A., 15
Salomon, G., 90
Salvadoran University Student Union (USEA), 65
Sameroff, A. J., 90
Sanders, M. S., 68
Saunders, M., 66
Scales, P. C., 2, 20
Schlozman, K., 18
Schwartz, S. H., 12, 16
Scotchmer, C., 82
Scott, T., 49
Seidman, E., 36, 37
Seif, H., 4, 5, 7, 59, 63, 64, 67, 68, 69, 75, 105
Selee, A., 60
Self and identity development, 16–17

Seligman, M.E.P., 16
Sellers, R. M., 53
Serpell, R., 5, 7, 77, 78, 79, 80, 82, 86, 88, 90, 93, 98, 103
Sesma Jr., A., 2
Share, R. A., 32, 35
Sherrod, C. A., 2
Sidanius, J., 48
Silva, C., 105
Silva, E., 105
Skoe, E. E., 19
Smetana, J. G., 16
Snyder, M., 20
Social dominance orientation (SDO), 48
Social incorporation, 3
Social Justice Education Project (SJEP), 31–32, 38
Social responsibility: Child-to-Child curriculum and, 85–86; conclusions on, 21–22; defining, 12–14; developmental origins of, 3–4, 14–17; empathy and, 15; opportunities to practice, 19–21; seedbeds of, 17–21; as a value, 12–13
Sociopolitical Control Scale (SPCS), 50
Sonn, C., 54
Sorenson, N., 98
Soukamneuth, S., 34
Speer, P. W., 30, 32, 38, 51
Spinrad, T. L., 15
Stacks, J. S., 32, 35
Stahlhut, D., 30
Stallworth, L. M., 48
Staples, L., 29, 34
Stepick, A., 53, 63, 64
Stepick, C., 53, 63
Stewart, S., 49
Stocks, E. L., 15
Stoecker, R., 28
Stoppa, T., 102
Stout, M., 13, 102
Student groups, immigrant, 68–69
Students Informing Now (S.I.N.) Collective, 69
Subramaniam, A., 97
Sullivan, P., 33, 98
Syvertsen, A., 3, 4, 7, 11, 13, 17, 19, 20, 25, 99, 102
Szalacha, L., 97

Takahashi, K., 105
Tan, D., 16
Tanaka, M., 49

Taylor, A. J., 103
Terriquez, V., 66
Tharp, R. G., 83
Tolman, J., 35
Toomey, R. B., 97
Torney-Purta, J., 2, 18, 63
Torres-Fleming, A., 28
Trahan, E., 46
Trickett, E. J., 35
Trost, C., 60
Trust in humanity, 13–14
Tseng, V., 37
Tucker, C. J., 14, 19, 103
Tuition laws, in-state, 67–68

Udell, C., 81
Uribe, F., 88

Valdes, P., 28
Valenzuela, A., 63, 64, 97
Valsiner, J., 90
Value messages from parents, 18–19
Vavrus, J., 34
Velez, V., 66
Verba, S., 18, 20
Verplanken, B., 13
Villalobos, M., 16
Voight, A. M., 4, 7, 32, 43, 57
Vygotsky, L. S., 83, 96, 103

Warren, M. R., 29, 34, 37
Watkins, N. D., 33, 98

Watts, R. J., 4, 7, 14, 32, 43, 46, 49, 55, 57
Westheimer, J., 14, 44
Westheimer, K., 97
Wilkenfeld, B., 63
Woodland, M., 81
Woodson, C., 45
Working memory, 15–16
Wray-Lake, L., 3, 4, 7, 11, 17, 19, 25, 99

Yang, K. W., 60, 72
Yates, M., 19, 20
Yescas, C., 71
Youniss, J., 19, 20
Youth Inventory of Involvement (YII), 50
Youth organizing: case examples of, 29–32; common elements of, 27, 32–34; conclusions on, 37–39; defined, 28; multilevel framework of, 35–37

Zaff, J., 13
Zahniser, J. H., 50
Zaman, W., 86
Zambian primary school, Child-to-Child approach at, 5, 77–91
Zehr, M. A., 38
Zeldin, S., 28, 29, 34, 35
Zimmerman, M. A., 46, 50, 53
Zone of proximal development, Vygotsky's, 83

Statement of Ownership

Statement of Ownership, Management, and Circulation (required by 39 U.S.C. 3685), filed on OCTOBER 1, 2011 for NEW DIRECTIONS FOR CHILD AND ADOLESCENT DEVELOPMENT (Publication No. 1520-3247), published Quarterly for an annual subscription price of $89 at Wiley Subscription Services, Inc., at Jossey-Bass, One Montgomery St, Suite 1200, San Francisco, CA 94104-4594.

The names and complete mailing addresses of the Publisher, Editor, and Managing Editor are: Publisher, Wiley Subscription Services, Inc., A Wiley Company at San Francisco, One Montgomery St, Suite 1200, San Francisco, CA 94104-4594; Editor, Co-Editor, Reed Larson, Univ. of Illinois, Dept. of Human Community Dev., 1105 W. Nevada St., Urbana, IL 61801; Managing Editor, Co-Editor- Dr. Lene Arnett Jensen, Clark University, Dept. of Psychology, 950 Main St., Worcester, MA 01610. Contact Person: Joe Schuman; Telephone: 415-782-3232.

NEW DIRECTIONS FOR CHILD AND ADOLESCENT DEVELOPMENT is a publication owned by Wiley Subscription Services, Inc., 111 River St., Hoboken, NJ 07030. The known bondholders, mortgagees, and other security holders owning or holding 1% or more of total amount of bonds, mortgages, or other securities are(see list).

	Average No. Copies Each Issue During Preceding 12 Months	No. Copies Of Single Issue Published Nearest To Filing Date (Summer 2011)
15a. Total number of copies (net press run)	689	696
15b. Legitimate paid and/or requested distribution (by mail and outside mail)		
15b(1). Individual paid/requested mail subscriptions stated on PS form 3541 (include direct written request from recipient, telemarketing, and Internet requests from recipient, paid subscriptions including nominal rate subscriptions, advertiser's proof copies, and exchange copies)	108	106
15b(2). Copies requested by employers for distribution to employees by name or position, stated on PS form 3541	0	0
15b(3). Sales through dealers and carriers, street vendors, counter sales, and other paid or requested distribution outside USPS	0	0
15b(4). Requested copies distributed by other mail classes through USPS	0	0
15c. Total paid and/or requested circulation (sum of 15b(1), (2), (3), and (4))	108	106
15d. Nonrequested distribution (by mail and outside mail)		
15d(1). Outside county nonrequested copies stated on PS form 3541	43	42
15d(2). In-county nonrequested copies stated on PS form 3541	0	0
15d(3). Nonrequested copies distributed through the USPS by other classes of mail	0	0
15d(4). Nonrequested copies distributed outside the mail	0	0
15e. Total nonrequested distribution (sum of 15d(1), (2), (3), and (4))	43	42
15f. Total distribution (sum of 15c and 15e)	151	148
15g. Copies not distributed	538	548
15h. Total (sum of 15f and 15g)	689	696
15i. Percent paid and/or requested circulation (15c divided by 15f times 100)	71.3%%	71.6%%

I certify that all information furnished on this form is true and complete. I understand that anyone who furnishes false or misleading information on this form or who omits material or information requested on this form may be subject to criminal sanctions (including fines and imprisonment) and/or civil sanctions (including civil penalties).

Statement of Ownership will be printed in the Winter 2011 issue of this publication.

(signed) Susan E. Lewis, VP & Publisher-Periodicals